"Mike McCann has written a book
that will make you laugh, even howl. It
will at the very least, stir your deeper
sensitivities and sometimes lay you open
to the marrow. Somehow he has managed
to squeeze every lemon that life has rolled
his way to make a powerful lemonade - a
combination of bold humor and deep insight
into the human condition. If you enjoy
reading at all, take a look at this wide
ranging collection of short stories.
Mike McCann's "Give Me the Hudson
or the Yukon" is one of a kind."

Sharon Nault,
Field Editor, The Milepost ®
1973-1984

"Two Days with Blackie" appeared in *Alaska Flying Magazine*, September 1987.

"Clean Sweep" appeared in *Outpost Magazine*, October 1987.

"Let's Change Seats" and "Old Blue" were published in *We Alaskans*, a supplement of the Anchorage Daily News, Spring 1989.

"Firewood on the River" appeared in *We Alaskans*, October 1989

"Flying Home the Bacon" was published in *Western Flyer*, August 1989. *Alaska Magazine*, September 1989 and in *We Alaskans*, November 1989.

Printed and bound in the USA.

ISBN 0-9627530-0-9

Published by:

Ridgetop Press

P.O. Box 1521

Homer, AK 99603

A special thanks to the Bozeman, Montana and Homer, Alaska writers' groups for their encouragement and enthusiasm. Also special thanks to Tricia Brown, Gwen Peterson and Shirley Timmreck.

Dedicated to the memory of our mother,
Kathleen Rudden
*in appreciation for her sharing her time,
humor and spirit of adventure with us.*

Give Me the Hudson or the Yukon

A Collection of Mostly *True Stories*

By Mike McCann

Ridgetop Press
P.O. Box 1521
Homer, Alaska 99603

Contents

Part I
Living on the Yukon River, Tanana, Alaska

Shanghai ————————————— 17
Clean Sweep ————————————— 25
Let 'em Stick ————————————— 29
Irish Rose ————————————— 33
Old Indian Trick ————————————— 37
Wrong Dead Man ————————————— 41
Deuces Wild————————————— 45
Out for a Paddle ————————————— 49
Race Time ————————————— 61
Just Like Stan ————————————— 73
Firewood on the River ————————————— 81

Part II
Flying in the North Country

Flying Home the Bacon ————————————— 89
"I'm Not Lost, Where Are We?"————————— 93
Two Days with Blackie ————————————— 99
Tail Heavy ————————————— 105
Hanging High————————————— 111
Old Blue ————————————— 117
A True Alaskan Experience ————————————— 124
Let's Change Seats ————————————— 133
Kinda Rough Landing————————————— 137
Fresh Melon ————————————— 139

Part III
Living on the Hudson River, New York

A New Dad —————————— 145

Fourth of July———————— 149

Ace Mechanic————————— 153

Rude Awakening ——————— 157

Pop the Clutch ——————— 159

Mr. Gillette ————————— 163

The Most Beautiful Girl in New York —— 171

Horse Corn————————— 175

What Rabbit?————————— 179

Thanks, Mom ————————— 183

Glossary ——————————— 197

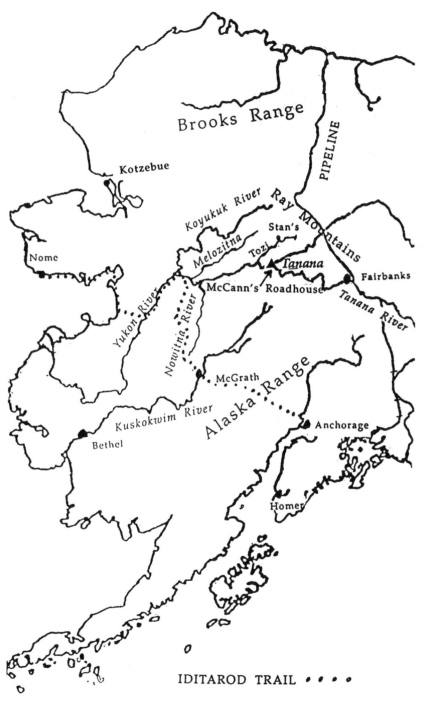

Brooks Range

Kotzebue

Koyukuk River

Ray Mountains

PIPELINE

Nome

Melozitna

Tozi

Stan's

Tanana

Fairbanks

McCann's Roadhouse

Yukon River

Nowitna River

Tanana River

McGrath

Alaska Range

Kuskokwim River

Anchorage

Bethel

Homer

IDITAROD TRAIL •••••

Part I

Living on the
Yukon River
Tanana, Alaska

Shanghai ─────────────────

The first patch of blue sky in weeks appeared to the south. "Here comes Eskimo summer!" I yipped, straddling the river log I used for my workbench as I sharpened a pile of saw chains. These chains needed to be like new so I could finish notching the corner logs on our new cabin.

"We may be in our new cabin sooner than we think." I grinned at my wife, Claire, who sat against the river bank, nursing Chris, our four-month-old son.

We both knew hope was thin. It had already snowed twice. My part-time job unloading the river barges had turned full-time, as every captain was racing to beat the ice. All this left me little daylight to work on our new home.

With Chris slung on my back and Claire alongside, we hiked the zigzagged mile on the narrow muddy trail to the hilltop where our half-finished home sat. It overlooked the Yukon and McKinley towered in the hazy distance. The structure, the usual crude sixteen-by-twenty-four foot, two-story log home, would normally take two or three months to build.

This one had already taken much longer due to its location - a beautiful spot high on the ridge above the river. The only drawback: no road and barely a trail that several of us had hand-hewed into the front slope.

We sledded most everything in from the north the previous winter, using a snow-packed tundra trail. We pushed and pulled sled loads with an ancient D-4 Caterpillar and large teams of sled dogs. Anything forgotten, or that was unavailable before spring thaw, had to be packed up the steep front trail. Already we had hauled floorboards, windows, even cement mix on our backs. Very often I wished I owned a helicopter.

Notching corners was my least favorite part of this project. By mid-afternoon I had completed all but two timbers. Hollering "Hallelujah!" I danced a little jig and gave Claire the thumbs-up sign. She was twenty feet away, folding insulation, Chris asleep on her back.

I poked my ear plugs in and yanked the pull cord, bringing my saw to life. Squatting in an unorthodox stance, my left arm slightly flexed, I used the blade tip for the first vertical cut. This would have been fine, except the log had a hidden knot, causing the saw to buck several times. Then it screamed full throttle and tore loose of my grip, forcing my left fist into the bridge of my nose. The chain gnawed full-speed into my forehead and scalp.

Stunned, deaf, with half a view, I leaned against a tree palming my right eye and brow as hard as I could.

My head felt like the ball in the winning home run of the World Series. A strong, wet pulse ran down my forearm, dripping into a pool off my elbow. Claire was screaming and waving a Pamper in my face. I wouldn't show her the wound, sure that if I had cut a spurter, she would faint.

Hoping the flow between my fingers would slow, I stalled Claire, asking dumb questions. "Are you sure that's not a used Pamper?" She got mad; I wouldn't let her see my new permanent part.

As the blood got sticky and my left eye started to clear, I thought, "No, I really don't want to be a prizefighter after all."

Still unsure of the status of my right eye, I meant only to comfort Claire by saying, "Honey, settle down, it's not my good eye." That was it. She pushed me down on the ground next to Chris, yelling, "I'm getting Bill."

Last I saw, this little woman running away full-speed with a big wet spot on her backside.

"Damn, she's excited," I thought. Luckily, Bill and Margaret were also building on the ridge a quarter-mile east of us. Bill, the only doctor for hundreds of miles in all directions, was a good friend and neighbor.

Within minutes, there was a crowd.

I would not release my pressure hand until we had discussed the options. Bill's sewing kit was four miles away at their house in the village. Our home was a mile hike downhill. Bill agreed I had two more hours of working daylight if the bleeding had stopped, but Margaret and Claire threatened to hog-tie and carry me down the hill.

Finally able to see light out of my right eye, I felt better, and put my right hand down, exposing the fresh wound. From their looks, I knew I was going down the hill. Now!

Pampered and staggering, I made it in the door as Bill and Margaret slid the kitchen table to the front window for more operating light. Margaret prepped and draped me for the latest in Bush plastic surgery.

The saw had cut from the eyelid well into the hairline and down to bedrock.

"Jesus," I thought, peeking into a small hand mirror. It looked much worse than I had imagined.

Margaret cleaned and pressured the cut. Bill, readying his equipment, said, "This is gonna take several hours; I got a lot of trimming to do on these jagged edges. Also, I have nothing to help stop the bleeding. If it continues at this rate through the procedure, you're gonna need to get into Fairbanks for a unit or two tomorrow."

"Whatever you say, Doc." I was totally confident with Bill, until halfway through the surgery. While restructuring my eyelid, he informed me that he had run out of Lidocaine, the local anesthetic. I gripped the table edge with both hands, chattering incessantly, a voice pitch change each time Doc cued me he was going for another eyelid stitch. Margaret, as assistant, suggested several times in her fresh Irish accent, "Bill, would ya sew up the man's lips so we can continue our work?"

I was startled as the phone rang on the window sill next to my head. Reaching my left hand from under blood-soaked drapes, I grabbed the receiver and slid it back under and up to my ear. It was Jack, my boss from Fairbanks.

"How's the inventory?" he hollered over our poor satellite connection. "You got all the oil ya need for winter?"

"No way. I need 100,000 more gallons, Jack," I yelled.

"Jack, I'm getting a face-lift. I'll call ya tomorrow."

The house meanwhile had filled with the usual summer evening crowd, each taking a turn holding and adjusting the small lamp while Bill sewed and lectured on the different stitches used for facial wounds. One voice belonged to John Hildebrant, a canoeist and writer from Wisconsin who had just pulled up to our dock, and had hesitantly volunteered to take a turn as surgeon's helper. The light roamed in his hands. Later he told me he'd nearly fainted. I was glad he hadn't joined me on the table.

The wound bled steadily into my scalp, the blood hardening to form a plaster-like hat that cracked each time I flinched. Bill finished me up, using two Pampers and an elastic Ace wrap to keep pressure on the wound. I adjusted to being upright.

The phone rang again. It was Joe Runyan, a fisherman who camped forty miles up the Yukon River in the summer.

"Mike, just in for supplies. There's three canoeists camped at the barge landing, looking for work. They spent the night at my fish camp. Seem like good hands - how's your new house going?"

"I could sure use some help. Thanks for the tip, Joe. I'll get down to the landing tonight. Take care."

Vertical and gift-wrapped, I looked like a sheik after a rough night at the Desert Inn Disco. Both eyes were swollen into slits, my neck was caked with dried blood.

I grabbed a visitor to drive my old Jeep and we made our way for the kitchen door. Margaret and Claire once again hindered my efforts, demanding that Bill tranquilize me.

"He doesn't have enough blood left. Besides, I don't know a thing that will touch him."

"Thanks, Bill. I just need some air, ladies."

"You don't need air," Margaret snapped. "You need a straight jacket."

Bumping down the trail minutes later, I had to agree.

We pulled up to their campfire at the barge landing. I climbed out of the old Jeep and introduced myself to the two college grads, Doug and Bill from Idaho, and a foot ball player, Jacques from Quebec.

"What type of work do you guys do?"

Doug spoke up. "We'll do anything. We've all done carpentry and cement work."

"Great. I'm trying to finish a cabin on the ridge east of town. Why don't you guys tie your canoe on the Jeep? We can make two trips for your gear, and you can camp up next to our house."

They looked at me. They looked at each other. I could feel the hesitation. Was it my new hat? I explained that there'd been an accident.

"I don't usually look like this, fellas - often worse." They smiled tightly.

It was getting late. I told them I'd check back early the next morning; they seemed relieved.

It hit me strange. Most canoeists jumped at the offer to

camp at our house, well-known as a halfway point down the Yukon River where folks were welcome. Yet these guys almost panicked when I made the offer.

It wasn't until three weeks later, as we were finishing the cabin roof, that Doug and Bill clued me in on why they hesitated at my invite that first evening. Doug started.

"The day before, we were up at Joe's fish camp asking about work on the river, Joe told us that you usually needed help and hired travelers. He said your nickname on the River was Shanghai, that you'd probably hire us and feed us well - warning us the only clincher was you liked to box. And often at your house you'd have knock-down, drag-outs before dinner."

Bill interrupted, "Yeah, Joe said Shanghai's from New York and calls it fun. The local Indians don't jump at the chance, so he recruits foreigners off the river."

This was the first I'd heard the story. Not that it wasn't true. I'd never realized that boxing stood out as a strange form of entertainment.

They both grinned, then Bill said, "Joe told us your favorites were the Germans because once you got them to put the gloves on and go a few rounds, several even delayed their trips a few days hoping to finish you off. He said,"If you guys are lucky, they'll be a few Krauts visiting and Shanghai might let you off light.'"

They explained in great detail how paddling that last forty miles they joked about who was gonna go first against me in the ring.

Bill's eyebrows went up. "Although we were definitely anxious about meeting you. Joe made it sound like you never lost. We pictured a real animal. And what steps into the firelight?"

"Nothin'," Doug cut in, "I mean NOTHING could a prepared us for the way you looked. That big blood spotted wrap on your head, your eyes black slits. Blood caked in your ears and beard."

"Damn, you looked wicked," Bill laughed. "You drove off, and we all sat there dead quiet, thinking exactly the same thing: "Man, this is the Twilight Zone. Let's get the hell out of here."

"We were convinced you made up that story about the saw accident just to get us up to your house."

"Yeah, we thought you'd probably been worked over bad and were really out for revenge. Sun up, we all kept saying it had to have been a nightmare."

Doug imitated how Jacques yelled that next morning when I drove up. "Oh, Christ here he comes, run for it."

They reminded me how I jumped out saying, "So you guys are ready to move up to the house - great! My wife has a big breakfast made, bear ribs and sourdough pancakes. And then we'll get hammering on the cabin."

"We all froze," said Bill. "Except our eyes bolting at each other."

"Well, you did look a little better..."

"And my mouth watered at the mention of bear ribs, especially after living two months on granola and freeze-dried soup."

"But the bear ribs were the catcher."

We sprawled on the roof having a good laugh. Bill lunged over and gave me a shot in the arm.

"Hey, we're sticking around 'til one of us finishes you off."

Clean Sweep _____

Hans was sick of eating fish. All he could talk about was getting a moose for the winter menu.

The only moose he'd ever seen was pickled and stuffed, standing in the Anchorage airport terminal.

"Are they all that big?" he asked. I couldn't tell him that one was a dehydrated munchkin compared to the bulls in this neighborhood.

"Naw. He's a big daddy," I reassured Hans, afraid if I told him the truth, he might hide his gun and go on a Hare Krishna diet for the winter.

Hans and Fleming had come from Denmark to canoe the Yukon River. We met half way into their river journey when they pulled their canoe up to my dock. They had already considered spending a winter in the Arctic Bush when I offered a stack of peeled, dry house logs I had cached at an old silver mine.

I suggested they return in the fall, when they completed their canoe trip. Then we could all pitch in and build a tight little cabin by freeze-up.

They returned in mid-September and promptly set in on building a new home at the mine, located a half-mile from the river on the wildest and most spectacular stretch of the

Upper Yukon.

"Four months of fish, three meals a day - boiled, baked, fried and smoked," Hans complained. "If I have to eat another bite of salmon, I'm going back to Denmark and live on chemicals again."

"Hans, we can't take time to go moose hunting."

I was ramrodding the cabin. If you haven't spent a winter in interior Alaska, it is impossible to imagine how fast winter hits - it seems to only take minutes.

"Hans, the moose will come knocking at your door. Don't sweat it," I constantly reassured him. "If we have to, we can run 'em down on snowshoes when the snow gets deep. But let's get the roof on!" By mid-October, it had already snowed twice.

The last two days on the cabin were spent digging the logs and tools out of the fresh snow so we could notch the roof purlins.

The Danes were finally tucked in for a winter on the Yukon. That evening at the house-warming, Hans raised his glass of Yukon Jack announcing, "It's gonna be rice and dried fish this winter." He had an extremely sad look.

By midnight there were two freshly emptied bottles of Yukon Jack. The Danes and their cabin were officially warmed.

The following morning was cold and bright. Hans spent his usual pre-oatmeal half hour on the Styrofoam throne he had built two hundred feet up the hill above the cabin. It was three-sided, leaving a panoramic view of the river. Hans had picked the spot and often said it made him feel like a king to sit with such a view of his imagined domain.

The bright light reflected off the snow as the previous evening's bottle of whiskey pushed heavy on Han's eyelids. He could barely manage a squint. His brain felt thick and sluggish, a lot like the oatmeal he would soon attempt to eat.

As his vison began to clear, Hans gasped. "Oh no, now

I'm hallucinating. Already Cabin Fever," he thought as he tried to focus on the biggest bull for miles.

The moose stood fifty feet away and stared at this bleary-eyed human crouching pantless in the three-sided box. Then the bull turned his head toward the cabin below and its crackling stove pipe. Hans snapped to.

Hobbled from the knees down, Hans hopped, tripped and rolled down the hill to the cabin. Yanking the door open, he babbled as if he'd just seen a ghost. He lunged for a rifle under the coat rack inside the door.

Hans turned and squatted into the ready position as he lined up for a shot. The moose hadn't moved, but was in little danger.

Hans was sighting in on him with a ragged old broom.

Fleming had the real gun and dropped the big bull almost in the frying pan.

Hans cussed and slammed the old broom against the cabin, splintering it into many pieces.

Then he felt the cold breeze, and bent over to pull up his trousers.

Let 'em Stick _____

Dan and Ellen were famous for just getting by. In my few months as a Bush hospital nurse, I'd heard many stories from the villagers about this young couple from Boston. They were the first to homestead in the Tozi River Valley, a desolate burned-off area fifty miles due north of the village of Tanana.

I heard that during their first season in the Bush, they built a cabin using less than a handful of rusty old nails; how they ate ravens more often than most urbanites eat chicken, along with a few surplus husky puppies to vary the menu. Their first summer diet consisted mostly of spawned-out salmon they found floating back downsteam in various stages of disintegration. Dan was unable to catch the spawning fish due to high water and lack of netting equipment.

That fall, word was out that I had redone an old cabin near the village, and had extra room and welcomed travelers. Sleeping space was scarce in the small village. Most families were packed into one-room cabins, with little room for an extra relative, let alone a rarely seen bushy traveler.

Homesteaders most often made their winter mail runs to town by dog team, squeezing errands, mail and visiting into one day, then back-tracking their trail to a protected camping spot.

Since the first heavy snow, I'd had many overnighters - some from as far as a hundred miles out, often on their first visit to town since the previous March when the spring thaw had knocked out the trails. Most were anxious to share their summer adventures while I sat entranced.

Sometimes several people would arrive in the same evening, and sit up until all hours sharing new techniques of surviving, or barely surviving, in the Arctic Bush.

The night I finally got to meet Dan and Ellen, they slid into my yard, each riding a runner behind a huge freight sled, which was pulled by twelve of the widest assortment of sled dogs I'd ever seen.

Ellen, a petite gal, wore a beautiful embroidered parka with a shiny black ruff and fancy caribou knee-high mukluks. Then she flipped back her hood and I thought, "This woman looks more like an uptown Second Avenue boutique owner than a Bush wife."

Dan looked more his part. Short, with a scraggly beard, he wore patch-quilted coveralls. His hat and ruff were blond, of a fur I didn't recognize. As he rocked back and forth on his mukluks, slapping his well-worn beaver mitts together, he reminded me of one of the seven dwarfs during choir practice.

We three pitched in to stake out the dogs and cut sprucebow beds for each trail-worn husky.

It was already forty below zero. A shivering dog will lose considerable weight and strength overnight, then be useless on the trail. A simple brush bed makes all the difference in keeping a dog off the snow - warm and rested. Then inside, crowded around the old barrel wood stove for a mug-up, Dan and I began swapping stories about being raised under the lights. He was from Boston and I, New York.

Excited, Ellen cut in.

"Dan, what about Cowgirl? How could we forget her?" Then, turning to me, "Mike, can I bring in our house pet?"

"Sure, Ellen, but it's not much warmer in here. I advertise space, not heat."

She darted outside. I expected her to return with a lead dog or other favorite team member, never the miniature white poodle that leaped from her arms at the doorway, then bounded for a seat near the stove. "Whoa!" I thought. "This can't be the same Dan and Ellen I've heard so many stories about. They're both spotless, compared to most trappers and homesteaders I've met. And now a poodle." I was sure this was another case of local conspiracy to buffalo the new male nurse.

Ellen held up a small sack of wheat flour.

"I'll make cookies while you guys catch up on history."

It was a treat having a woman in the kitchen after eight months of trappers, fishermen, Indians and drunks in all combinations.

Then she needed oil.

"The only oil I have goes in my chainsaw or sno-go."

"Don't be funny, Mike. I need something to keep the dough from sticking to the pan."

"Sorry, Ellen. Don't have a thing."

For several minutes, she shuffled along the one shelf I called a kitchen.

I caught a contemplative look turn into a dead-eyed stare. "I noticed that old dog Tiger that Russ gave you in September isn't in your dog yard. What happened to him?"

"He was too old and slow, didn't make it past Thanksgiving. He's out back in the pile with the rest of the sled dogs that got an early trip to doggie heaven," I said like an old sourdough.

She stepped toward Dan and bent to unhook his belt knife.

"Just where is that pile of dogs? I'll whack off a small chunk from his frozen fat neck."

Her eyes gleamed commitment. She was buttoning her parka!

I jumped in front of the door.

"Please, Ellen!" I begged. "Let the cookies stick!"

Now I could see how Dan and Ellen always got by. But this time, Ellen wasn't getting by me.

Irish Rose

She was a real Irish Rose.

Margaret, the new doctor's young wife, came from Dublin. Dolled to the nines, rosy cheeks, flour-white skin, the latest in jewelry and fashionable dress. It was a pleasure to have someone so up-to-date in the village. Tanana (population 350; dogs 1,200), halfway down the Yukon River from the Canadian border, was inhabited mostly by dog-crazed Native fishermen and trappers.

Dr. Bill and Margaret lived on the hospital compound in a two-story modern gray house overlooking the river. The compound is located on the downriver side of the small rustic community with its many log cabins and large sled dog yards.

Bill jumped in with both feet, building a dog sled and collecting a team his first winter, then renting a cabin four miles from the village.

In early February my wife, Claire, and Margaret planned a sled trip north to visit homesteaders Russ and Ann, forty miles north of Tanana. The ladies hitched up two eight-dog teams and packed their sleds.

It was minus 40 degrees when they slid out of the yard behind the barking hounds. Bill and I escorted them by snowmachine for the first few miles in case any of the team members tangled. Controlling a frisky team when one member is being dragged or twisted in the lines can only maim a good dog.

We stopped the snowmachines when it looked as if all was under control. The women faded off down the trail with the two strings of loping sled dogs.

Bill looked concerned.

"Hey, they'll be okay. You'd have more reason to worry if Margaret were driving a snow machine." I tried to sound reassuring. "They can always eat a dog if they get stranded."

Bill rolled his eyes and hung on to the serious look. I didn't want to let on, but I was impressed. There was Margaret, the latest and most civilized addition to town, off by dog team across the tundra on a brisk February morning.

I never ceased to be amazed at the transition many people would go through when they reached such an isolated community. Locals watched and often took bets on newcomers. How long would they last, or what faction would they join after six months. Drinkers and Bible-thumpers were the two main categories. Then there were dog mushers, fishermen, trappers and airplane fanatics.

Margaret was already an extreme case by my book. The Irish Rose mushing off across the tundra.

It was now the last week in April. I was rushing to get my oil deliveries done before the roads went soft, and my old 2,000-gallon tanker truck sank out of sight.

When the days lengthen and the warm wind blows in Interior Alaska, the snow goes quickly, the mud deepens. It's also the time when many items appear that you haven't seen since last September - boats, motors, tools, garbage emerge from the snow melt.

One sunny April morning, my truck lugged up the long gradual climb to the last cabin on the old site road. It was 8 a.m. when I crept by Bill and Margarets' cabin. I heard a chainsaw echoing from behind their house. Knowing Bill had flown out to do temporary duty in Fairbanks, I was curious and concerned. I'd become extra sensitive about running chainsaws since Bill sewed up my forehead the past fall. The result of a kickback accident.

I shut down the truck and jumped out. The saw wailed, barely letting up. I thought someone had to be cutting a big log, with long runs like that. If it was Margaret, I'd cut in and offer to help. If someone else was volunteering or working for her, fine, I'd ease back out of the yard.

Rounding the corner of the cabin, there was Margaret. Plaid skirt, pretty scarf wrapped tightly under a set of earmufflers. She was bent over, using her left boot as a brace. I crept closer, not wanting to startle her. I'd rather sneak up on someone with a bazooka than a chainsaw.

There were pieces of fur, not bark, in the air. Margaret let off the trigger and kicked a chunk as the saw wound down.

"Margaret!" I shouted from several feet away. She flicked the kill switch and peeled off her headset. I could see she already had her rouge and eye make-up on. Little balls of fur were stuck to her expensive Aran sweater.

Figuring she had caught an old caribou hide with the saw, I asked, "What's all the fur?"

"Ah, the mister goes off and leaves me with this pile of frozen dogs. As soon as the sun hits this snow bank, these beasts are gonna stink!" She then grabbed a grayish hindquarter by the paw and yanked it loose. With a pop, the hip socket let go. Turning, with her free hand, she lifted a plywood lid off a 50-gallon drum of boiling dog food, and tossed it in. The leg floated to the top among the brown rice and salmon chunks she was cooking for the live members of her team.

Margaret continued her tirade as she swept flecks of dog fur off her sweater. I stood with my mouth open (not real wide, there was fur everywhere).

Shrugging her shoulders, she said, "Someone's gotta do it, can't waste these old hounds." She pointed to a snowpile that had a few canine limbs poking out.

I slowly walked back to the truck, shaking my head. The Irish Rose had just topped 'em all.

Old Indian Trick _____

The old diesel Cat looked dead to me. Her tracks were sagging. The hoses were cracked and leaking hydraulic oil. A solid coat of rust covered her frame.

For years, she had been hidden among the alders behind my shop in downtown Tanana, a two-car Indian village on the north bank of the Yukon River.

I phoned Jim, the Cat's owner, who now lived in Nenana, a village on the Tanana River. I explained I was cleaning up the shop yard and offered to haul his heap to the dump. Jim was highly insulted and let me know loud and clear that his Cat was just like new, ready to crank anytime. Also that he'd be down to load it on the barge soon.

"Jim, when was the last time it ran?" I hated to ask.

"Just last year." He tried to sound convincing. Jim had been in a bad plane wreck last winter, and spent two days on the tundra waiting rescue. His left leg hadn't worked right since the accident, so I volunteered to try cranking the old Cat and loading it on the next barge to Nenana.

Jim accepted. I killed two birds with one phone call - cleaning up the yard as well as getting to work on some old equipment, a favorite hobby of mine. This piece looked as if it were built before the discovery of the wheel.

I chopped the thick alder limbs away from the tracks and undercarriage, wrapped two logging chains around the rear axle and hooked onto my tanker truck. The Cat wouldn't budge. I topped off my tanker truck with 2,000 gallons of diesel for extra weight and tried again. In super-low gear, the old Cat followed me out of the brush.

With a loud clack, clack, the loose track pads were flapping. I towed the heap in front of the shop for easy access to air tools and power.

It didn't take ESP to read the stares from local Indians walking by on the main road. "Uh-oh, McCann's got some more junk to tear apart." I thought to put a sign up: This is not mine.

A busy afternoon of cleaning filters, injectors, tightening the tracks and adjusting the steering clutches, new fuel and charged batteries. I'd worked through dinner, hoping this machine was ready to pop.

As I was ready to test it, an audience arrived: Richard, the power plant manager from Los Angeles, and Dave, a local fix-it man, preacher and Oklahoma refugee. Both had more diesel experience than I did, so I welcomed their input.

Mounted on the seat, clutch lever in hand, I pushed the starter button. Nothing but a click. Not even a groan. I was suddenly tired of this project. It was almost dark and I'd continue tommorrow.

Richard and Dave's enthusiasm picked up where mine left off. Dave already was hooking the thick chain around the Cat's front cross-beam. In his thick Oklahoma drawl, he commanded, "Mike, now back the truck up, and we'll jump-start this critter."

Rich had been a tank driver for three years in Vietnam. He hopped up on the seat and straddled the shift lever. I caught the thumbs-up sign in my side mirror and eased the clutch out. To start the truck rolling, I had to race the engine. A loud "clack, clack" could be heard as we accelerated easily for a six-ton tow.

Rolling along, I had a white-knuckle grip on the steering wheel, knowing it couldn't go this smoothly. I was sure when Richard released the Cat's clutch that my bumper was going to tear off. Even with several good bucks and lurches, we were still rolling, Cat in tow.

When darkness set in, I could barely make out my friends or the Cat. Suddenly a lurch and long steady tug, while an orange glow lit up the entire area. I could see Dave, wide-eyed, staring up with his mouth open like it might be the second coming. Then a blob of flaming lava-like glob landed with a splat two feet from my running board. I panicked and tried accelerating to get away from this shower of burning whatever.

The faster I went, the brighter the glow got. I was afraid to slow down with all these flames falling. In my mirror, it looked like New York's Fourth of July fireworks display. The hollering became desperate now. I slowed the truck and jumped out to find both Richard and Dave short of breath and standing ten feet back from the Cat's glowing molten exhaust stack.

The last globs of flames were being stamped out by kids who were now gathered around us. "Do it again, again," they cheered - like we had planned this torchlight parade. Many of the villagers had been drinking and now stood along the roadside with their beer cans held high in a toast.

We waited for the stack to cool while we poked at the piles of goop that were hardening on the road. I was the local authority on fuels: "It looks like flaming dinosaur poop to me."

"No, it's paint," Dave interjected. "Someone filled the stack with old paint." It did make sense, since kids were always playing around the shop.

"It's almost all burnt off," he said. "Now she'll run. Mike, let's go."

I wasn't in a hurry to be chased down Main Street by a shower of flying flame balls, so I stalled. But realizing I was about to lose my help, I gave in.

We were a half-mile from home. I started slowly and kept it that way, figuring the Cat wouldn't flame up as much. I lucked out. She leaped and lurched, but no more sparks. We were almost in the yard.

I heard a steady purr as the drag on the truck let up. I leaped from the cab, ran back and jumped up on the Cat's left track. Dave and Rich were hooting and racing the engine. There were no sparks, and it sounded great.

Dave wore a sly grin like he had a secret. Rich's arms were over his face. Thick black smoke poured from, from where? The intake. But that doesn't make sense, my brain told me. It's supposed to come out through the stack.

I checked the gear lever. It was in the reverse position. But I had been pulling the Cat forward. How could it start in reverse gear?

In response to my confused look, Dave casually said, "Old Oklahoma Indian trick. Sometimes these old Cats run better backwards." Then he burst into a yuk-yuk seizure.

Dave had the engine running backwards - a trick that's only possible with two-cycle diesel engines. Air was rushing in the exhaust stack, and smoke was pouring out the air filter. It now had one forward gear, which was labeled reverse, and four reverse gears labeled forward.

Rich drove forward in reverse, then backed around the yard in third forward, the fastest backing-up a Cat has ever performed.

It was late; I'd seen enough. Originally, I'd moved to the Alaskan Bush to simplify my life. I could see with friends like Dave and Richard, that would be impossible.

Wrong Dead Man _____

The village was on an extended drunk, thanks to uncontrolled state grants and Native dividend checks. Tommy was the number-two casualty from this Alaskan party.

He should not have died from a shot in the ass. Except the .22 bullet bounced repeatedly off the inner pelvic walls severing his descending aorta. During the one-hour Medivac flight, Dr. Bunde and I administered four liters of intervenus fluid, while Tom's blood pressure steadily faded.

There was no place for a tourniquet.

It was potlatch season, as many in the village had spent a busy summer boozing heavy. Tom's was in fact the third potlatch in two months. A Potlatch being the way the Athabascans of interior Alaska pay respect and say good-bye to the deceased - three days of eating and visiting the family, a church service, then burial and a large feast and dance at the community hall.

I had been to many during my time as a nurse in the Alaskan Bush. However this one was going to be different as Squashy, a close friend from my old New York neighborhood, was up visiting.

Squashy, a handsome Polish buddy, worked in the moving business since high school. In New York, the word was if Squash can't lift it, hire a crane. Built like Popeye, he carries a heart of gold.

In detail, I explained the potlatch tradition, how we should visit the family and share a meal before the burial. Squashy was game.

He always looked forward to meeting new people. In his few days in the village already he stood out as a very personable fellow. Several boatloads of Natives made the three-mile trip upriver to my house to visit the outgoing high-speed talker from New York.

The following day at noon, Squashy and I visited Tommy's parents at home. There were Indians of all ages, eating quietly, outside in the grass. An old woman motioned us to sit at the kitchen table as we entered the small, one-room tilted cabin. I felt honored, but could see in Squashy's face that he was a little spooked.

The cabin was crowded with mostly old folks speaking their Native tongue. We each were served a large plate of whitefish eggs, smoked salmon strips and a chunk of greasy beaver meat. This diet was new to Squash. He did well, even eating the skin off the salmon strips - something I'd never seen done before.

Suddenly Squashy's face went white as he quickly blessed himself and gave me the let's-go-quick head motion. I made the excuse that I had to show my friend to the outhouse, and would be right back. When we stepped out of hearing distance behind the cabin, Squash was talking with everything but his toes.

"Mike, that guy ain't dead. I saw him move. Don't let them bury him, I swear I ain't crazy." He went on and on, waving his arms as he tried to convince me.

"Ah, be serious, Squash. He's history. I was there when he died." I played along, knowing well that Tommy was on ice in the village morgue. It was Terry, Tommy's older brother, who Squash had seen flinch. He often looked dead and now dozed on a rickety cot in the back corner of the cabin, looking especially dead on this occasion.

It took a while, but I finally convinced Squashy it was totally disrespectful to leave our meals unfinished. He made me promise we'd then go immediately and report his discovery to Dr. Bunde.

We returned to our seats. Squashy snorfed the meal, his eyes never left the cot. Finished, he headed for the door, pausing only to say thank you and shake hands with Tommy's mom. He sneaked one last glance over her shoulder just as Terry rolled from the cot and thumped onto the floor.

That did it. Squashy launched for the door and slammed his head into the jam, which is saying something.

Squashy is only five foot six.

Deuces Wild

Maxim spoke little English. I didn't know any Cree.

So we spent our first evening together, playing cards in his small cabin on the Wabasca River.

We had met earlier that day. I was repairing an old cabin on the riverbank. I sensed a visitor, and looked up to find a stocky white-haired Indian with a wide smile standing in the doorway.

Introductions included twenty minutes of us both pointing, nodding and grinning. Finally I guessed that I was invited to dinner downriver that evening. After a bone crunching handshake, my new friend jogged down the riverbank trail in his high-top moosehide moccasins, rifle over his shoulder.

Two large bowls of steaming beavertail soup sat on the table when Max answered the door that evening. Another Rocky Marciano handshake, and I was barely able to hold onto the spoon handle. The soup was good. I avoided looking at the shiny black chunks that reminded me of pieces of a tire, tread and all.

Then they were all that was left. Max repeated, "Me-as-sin, Me-as-sin." I hoped that meant good. I stuck my fork into my first chunk of greasy beavertail. Better than I expected, I thought, nodding my approval. I chewed and chewed, encouraged to like the menu. I planned to stay in the country for the winter.

Before the table was cleared, Maxim set out a well-worn deck of cards. "Deuces Wild," he said clearly with a wide wrinkled smile. I was glad to see we had a couple more words in common.

During the game, Max often jumped up and shuffled off to a dark corner of the cabin, where he would dig in an old trunk or box then return with a fancy pair of beaded mocassins, vest or gun scabbord.

As my eyes widened, his pace increased until, along with pictures of his many grandchildren, the table and nearby floor was covered with his collection.

We played for hours. Most of the time the only sound was the slight hiss of the coal oil lamp or crackle of the wood stove.

My visible world was Max's deep wrinkled bronze face, snow-white hair and giant paws holding the cards in the soft lamplight.

While Maxim stoked the stove, I went outside to stretch. The October full moon polished the river's surface. From the bank it looked like a band of Christmas tinsel winding off into oblivion.

When I heard Max close the stove lid, I ducked back in through the narrow doorway.

We picked up our cards and continued. The stove's warmth smothered the chill that had begun to set in. I slipped into a state of suspended awakeness, thinking it couldn't get much better than this. Good company, a warm cabin on a river few ever heard of, the full moon overhead.

Suddenly.

A loud crack! Then snap! Snap! Rapid fire. Bullets were ricocheting off the walls, zinging all around us.

Max and I bumped rear-ends under the small table. I caught my breath and glanced at the windows. The glass was intact. The shots had to be coming through the narrow planked door.

After what seemed like hours, the firing stopped. Max was talking loudly in Cree. He must be telling them off, I thought.

Then Maxim began to get up. His hand over his mouth he was hissing between words. Max peeked above the table's edge, and the lamplight showed tear streams from both eyes. I didn't get it and wasn't about to move.

Then Max held up a small piece of lead and pointed at the woodstove. Which now had many bright red, glowing holes in its side. He tiptoed over and lifted its lid. In the firelight, Max bent over showing me how a handful of .22 shells had rolled from his shirt pocket into the fire during his last stoking.

Holding up a loaded shell, he laughed hard saying, "Deuces wild."

I slowly crawled out from under the table.

Out for a Paddle

Rich sold Italian wheelchairs in New York City, his first year out of college.

Over the phone, he moaned, "Mike, the selling is not so bad. It's reading the obituaries in the papers every morning. So then I can go track down the deadman's sad relatives and make an offer on a chair I probably just sold them a week ago. It's not a cheery business and my boss is this little greasy sleazeball. I don't doubt he turns his headlights off in the pedestrian crossing for more business."

"Rich, take a break. Come up to Alaska for a couple weeks. We'll do something different," I offered.

I was ready for a break myself. I'd worked the past year as a registered nurse in the Anchorage, Native Health Intensive Care Unit.

Rich and I had been friends since second grade. We competed on the same football and wrestling teams through high school. Often still, we tussle it out like brothers. His Rocky Marciano build against my longer-limb leverage always makes for a long match.

I signed us up for a fourteen-day shakedown kayak trip in Prince William Sound. The deal being, we would pay our expenses and help do grunt work setting up camps so we could be with two experienced guides. They were mapping a new route for clients that summer.

Eddy - balding, short, with a scrubby beard - appeared to have just traded his Jewish ringlets and trench coat on 47th Street in the New York Diamond District for a kayak paddle. Reilly was dark-haired, tall and tan, a recently retired Navy weather man. If he were standing next to a Wooden Indian, it would be hard to guess which had the pulse. They were to be our guides and bosses.

The morning of departure was sunny and crisp. At 6 a.m. we met at Lake Hood float plane dock. Then we loaded two weeks of gear and two folding Klepper kayaks into the Cessna 185.

The trip in was a spectacular hour and a half of flying between mountains, over glaciers, to a narrow spit of gravel jutting out in front of the Nellie Wan Glacier.

Erecting one of these kayaks was no snap. Our heap of ribs, stringers and rubberized cloth finally looked like a boat about noon.

Agreed our test row should be in as horizontal water as possible, Rich and I each grabbed an end and packed kayak and paddles over the spit to the calmer glacial lake. After twenty minutes, we were still upright and dry. We had it down.

The scenery was outrageous. Large sapphire blue ice chunks floating, with seals stretched out sunning themselves. All backed by a half-mile wide wall of glacier hundreds of feet high.

We paddled up close to the wall for a photo. As Rich clicked his camera, there was a loud crack.

"Oh-h-h-s-h-h-it!" we sang in harmony.

Digging in, we tried to speed away. A four-foot wave, from a fallen ice chunk, caught us broadside, half filling the Klepper with frigid water. Then all was quiet, except for the crackling as the small bergs bumped in the rippled lake. It sounded like a large bowl of Rice Crispies.

We were both bailing ice water with cupped hands, pulses racing. Then a roar.

"Please," I thought. "Be a sonic boom just this once." I glanced back. It looked like the Pan Am Building coming down Park Avenue.

Paddles flailing like bees' wings, we tried to fly. No such luck. The wave of this overgrown ice cube was eight feet high when it reached our stern. It launched us across the berg-filled lake. Rich guided the bow between the treacherous floaters. Within a breath we were deposited on the far edge of the spit. We jumped from the tiny boat. The lake was now a frothed mass of crunching icebergs.

Rich stared back into the lake and matter-of-factly said, "I'm calling a cab outta here."

Eddy was running full speed down the beach toward us. "Here comes Curly," Rich mumbled. Eddy arrived, short of breath, with a nervous face on, puffing, "I tried. I tried hollering at you guys...not to go so close to the ice wall."

His brow was covered with beads of sweat. I read his mind. Over and over he thought, "I almost lost these two rookies in the first hour, and we still have two weeks to go. Dear God."

Rich spoke up. "Eddy, I don't get it. That glacier has been sitting there for thousands of years. Why the hell does it start falling apart now?"

Eddy shrugged his shoulders and shook his head, refusing to answer, hoping Rich was only joking. We all pow-wowed on the beach around the pile of food and equipment.

Reilly informed us that the plan was to load up with equal weight in each kayak, paddle close to shore for a five hour stop and set up camp. Do this for two weeks with a day or two of rest. We should then have a route mapped out through the wildest and most spectacular coastal area of Alaska.

Loaded up, Reilly and Eddy had the food bags, Rich and

I, tents and gear.

A fine drizzle had started, we stretched a rubberized splash cover over each kayak. With help steadying the boat, Rich and I climbed in, cinching the apron tightly around our waists. We launched. Our loaded kayaks floated a few inches lower and felt more stable.

Our paddling became somewhat synchronized as we tried to keep up with our companions. It didn't take long to realize this was work. Although it felt like we were moving with each stroke, you could look up after hours and the islands that you spotted earlier seemed to be in the exact same spot - we learned to go from rock to rock.

The water was frigid. If you dipped in a hand while paddling, it went blue on the third stroke. This fact did help us keep balanced.

Rich reassured me with his commentary. He said, "Yep, sure like these splash covers. When you tip over, your feet don't get wet. You can't get out of the boat, that's a minor drawback, but at least when they find us upside down and dark blue, they might recognize the feet!" That was his positive thought of the day.

Wildlife was thick. Eagles soared low overhead. Otters cruised by on their backs. Small black-tailed deer bounded along the beaches. I thought we were in a Walt Disney movie.

We stopped for late lunch in a small cove. I looked forward to a big campfire with hot dogs and marshmallows. Wrong again. Eric fired up this tiny gas burner. It was so small, I could not imagine a pot on top without squashing it. Rich offered his Bic lighter to cook with. Within minutes the midget stove did its thing and we had hot lentil soup for four. Along with a handful of fruit mix that looked more like bird food, but tasted great. For dessert, a sesame seed bar that belonged in a parakeet cage.

It was all new and exciting! Rich asked Eddy if his family

ran a health food store. Eddy informed us he and Reilly were vegetarians and that this was all pure energy food.

I didn't realize until now that we had no meat - even - dried meat - among the groceries. My stomach flinched. The only item I recognized during our meal was a chunk of cheese.

A few exercises and wrestling on the beach before we loaded up and we were on our way. It didn't take all day to realize why I wasn't born an Eskimo. I had blisters covering both hands. They made it feel like trying to hold onto a handful of jellybeans and paddle at the same time. I dipped them in the cold saltwater for burning relief.

Rich and I would paddle hard, get way ahead of Eddy and Reilly, then jump out on the beach and flex our lower limbs.

The first week went about the same each day. We'd paddle four or five hours, set up a campsite, plot sites and alternates.

The lentils were getting old. We ate enough sesame seed bars to sprout feathers. Rich and I tried to hijack a foodbag into our boat - lucking out occasionally with the cheese stash.

My meat craving had peaked. I was dreaming about hamburgers and greasy fries. Rich threatened to wave a float plane down and order lasagna and pastrami.

Late evening, we sat huddled around a campfire. There was a rustle and flutter in a nearby spruce tree. Rich grabbed a handful of rocks and stalked instinctively.

The plump spruce hen was perched on a limb twenty feet up. Rich let fly a speedball that severed the hen's head clean off. The body fell to the ground and flapped, running along the beach. We spooked as the headless critter ran wildly for minutes, during which time I seriously considered joining the vegetarians.

That was until the aroma from the stew pot permeated. It was like Thanksgiving, the bird in the cooker. Rich and I devoured the mini-turkey past the marrow, leaving only feathers as evidence.

With the combination of lentils and wild meat, Rich and

I slept outside the small tent, hoping it wouldn't rain.

Now we were hunters. But word must have gotten out in the bird world, because that was the last grouse we saw. The two slingshots we fashioned out of a new pair of suspenders were only toys the rest of the trip.

Finally the clouds lifted the second week. Razor-edged mountain peaks were illuminated emerald green by the bright sunshine. High meadows severed by snowslides that sloped down to the waterline. My neck was stiff from looking up at this incredible arena.

The second sunny day, a headwind picked up, making it a struggle to keep the kayaks off the rocks. We agreed on pulling into a small cove for lunch.

Rich and I were a mile ahead of Eddy and Reilly. We turned towards the narrow inlet that opened into a glassy well-protected cove. I yelled, "Gold, Rich, gold!" and pointed at the glittering beach. "It's covered." We paddled hard, forcing the nose of the boat well into the sand. The two of us jumped out of the Klepper and pranced around our find.

The tide was coming in, so we had to make a move. On hands and knees, we scraped the fine layer with hunting knives, then dumped it into our gallon water jugs.

Eddy and Reilly were skeptics, but joined in all the same. We spent hours collecting and filled all possible containers with this shiny fine gold dust.

Marking the site on our maps, we discussed early retirement and investments. On the sly, Rich and I planned to move the X on Eddy's map so the cove didn't get too crowded in the future. From what I hear, this was normal behavior among gold prospectors.

The tide came in, covering our new mining claim. All three-gallon containers were full so we broke for lunch debating whether we should pack the kayak with our latest precious metal. Eddy kaboshed this idea promptly stating, "These Kleppers weren't designed to haul dirt."

Topping off another Hare Krishna lunch with a parrotstick (sesame bar), we repacked the boats. Both rode lower with the gallons of payload; neither wanted to leave on shore. Slowly we glided out of the cove into the choppy sound. The afternoon paddle went by fast, leaving us at a small beach on Applegate Island, where we agreed to take a day for R & R.

After breakfast the next morning, Rich and I paddled our unloaded kayak around the island. A treat - only one of us needed to paddle at a time, and we skimmed right along.

When we caught sight of the new campsite, I heard a sound like the air brakes releasing on a train or a steam valve popping. We sat still. All was quiet. Then suddenly the sound was closer. Behind us out of the corner of my eye, I saw four narrow, long fins surface less than 100 feet from our rear. "Sharks!" Rich screamed. We paddled madly, huffing and not looking back. The kayak flipped 20 feet from shore, dunking us into the frigid sound. I was sure we were goners. I tried running on the bottom without any luck.

We made it to shore. Eddy and Reilly were laughing out of control as we stripped down and ran naked up and down the gravel beach to warm up. The fins passed by within yards. Eddy clicked many pictures, then informed us they were harmless killer whales, or Orcas.

Rich smirked, "Just killer whales, huh? I don't like the name." Eddy reassured us, hoping he could convince us to eventually get back in the kayak since we were on an island and Rich had mentioned walking to Anchorage. As the whales faded into the distance, we suddenly realized we were bare-assed and began oh-ah-oh-ahing up to the campsite. Our guides were still chuckling at us two tender foots.

A three-mile crossing was next. We were not anxious to get back in the kayak, but we were encouraged by the fact that this would be the last wide-open water we had to paddle. Then we could hug the shoreline for the last two days into Whittier, our final destination.

The sea was smooth as a mirror during the crossing. We paddled hard and steady, then finally relaxed when the shoreline was within a hundred yards. The sun's reflection and heat was hypnotic. We laid back and waited for the others. Heads back, paddles across our laps, the only sound was the tiny drips off the paddle tips.

Rich faked a few snores then sighed, "This is the life, relaxing with a boatload of gold and not a worry. Can't beat ..." Before he could finish, there was a loud whoosh only a few feet in front of us. We both bolted upright like twin Siamese jack-in-the-boxes. We gasped simultaneously at the biggest, ugliest face I'd ever seen. It blew a wad of snot into the air, sounding like a fat man on a park bench.

The thing looked part bulldog, part grizzly bear with long fangs and big whiskers. Coming straight for us, it submerged slowly five feet from the tip of our boat. Finally able to speak, I screamed, "Paddle, Paddle." We didn't know whether to back up or go forward. Digging in full throttle, we made for shore. I knew this thing would come up from underneath and flip us any second. It seemed like hours to reach the shore, time enough for my life to flash by several times along with editing.

On shore, hearts pounding, "What the... what the hell was that," Rich spat out, hunched over and short of breath. Shaking his head, "New York, New York is much safer - that was the grossest face I ever saw! No way am I getting back in that boat."

"Rich, I think we're reacting to all the health food. It had to be an hallucination." I tried to sound convincing, hoping it really was.

Eddy just scrunched his brow as we explained in stereo,

along with sign language about the creature. "It was a sea lion. He's way more afraid of you guys." He grinned.

He didn't look afraid, that's for sure. We must look real bad if we can scare something that ugly.

It took more than coaxing, but Rich and I did get back in the kayak, never paddling more than 15 feet from shore and not relaxed for a second. My head constantly rotated 360 degrees, like an owl's.

Down the home stretch, a fifteen-mile narrow into Whittier, a storm blew hard, almost forcing us into the rocks. A short sandy stretch appeared. We pulled in and set up camp. Two days later, the storm still wouldn't back off. We were low on bird food and very tired of each other's company.

Over a bowl of what I believed to be off the bottom of a bird cage with powdered milk, Eddy informed us we would have to go on a survival menu.

"A what?" Rich and I met eyes.

"We're low on grub and stranded indefinitely but there's lots of edible plants right around camp," he assured us.

"Oh yeah, like what. Bark soup?" Rich joked sarcastically.

"Actually, birch cambian makes good soup," Reilly volunteered.

"I prefer toe-jam sandwiches," was my input. This wasn't gonna be fun. I could tell. We thought we'd been on a survival diet the past two weeks, and barely survived as it was.

Two and a half days of sauteed fiddlehead ferns and clams later, I knew if I ever saw another fern it would be way too soon.

Tied up to the dock in Whittier, civilization never looked so good, even if it was only a boat dock and train platform.

We folded up the Kleppers and repacked for the short train ride into Anchorage. Before hopping aboard, I turned to look down the long narrow fjord we had paddled. It was still spectacular. I hoped to return soon in a "bigger boat."

The Alaska Railroad slowly bumped and jerked along Turnagain Arm into Anchorage. We weren't in any big hurry, enjoying the two hours to relax and reminisce a bit about the past twenty-one days. None of us said a word. At the station in downtown Anchorage, we all shook hands and agreed to meet for a slide show.

Rich and I hoofed it to Burger King. I'll take a charred burger and some refried fries. It was time to grease up again. Although I did have a tinge of guilt.

"They almost converted us, Rich, but the fiddlehead ferns were the clincher for me."

"I was just getting to like those myself." He smiled.

Eight a.m. prompt, we arrived at the assayer's door with a jug of gold. It would be a few hours until he could confirm the percent and quality of our find.

We took a hike around Lake Hood, the largest float plane dock in Anchorage, trying to decide what type of aircraft we would need to travel to and from our gold claim.

We decided on either a Palatis Porter - Single Otter or Beaver on floats. Now with that narrowed down, a stop at the boat dealer, operations base could be from a large cabin cruiser in the small cove.

Life had sure gotten interesting. At 1 p.m., after another big lunch at Blubber King, we raced to pick up the results.

A big bald gent stood behind the counter smiling as we nonchalantly barged through the door. Rich tripped over a magazine rack as we tried to be cool and collected, then leaned against the counter. Like we do this all the time.

"Can you give us some numbers, sir?"

"Not really fellas." The Ajax man was still smiling.

"If you need more time we'll come back, no rush." Rich got out real smooth-like, then looked over at me and scrunched his eyebrows closer together.

"Nope, the test is all done. But there's only one way I

can explain clearly how much gold you brought in here this morning."

Just the word gold pumped us up. Beaming and in harmony we said, "Well, lay it on us."

"Okay, to be honest, there is actually more gold in the air we breath than there was in that container."

Ha Ha. We all had a good laugh - figuring he used the same line on everyone just for a joke. Hoping so.

Then he held out the typed report. .0001% - not a lot of gold.

We still have the X on the map, but decided we'd leave the claim for a while, kind of like money in the bank. We have gold on the beach. No reason to rush the work part - we know it's there, and we can still afford to dream.

Rich returned home to New York to find his boss at the wheelchair company had been deported. He joined the N.Y.P.D. and now works as an undercover agent in the South Bronx. Rich doesn't worry about glacier walls falling on him or killer whales popping up. But every time we get together, he suggests taking another Alaskan kayak trip.

Race Time _____

Claire finished handing out the Christmas mail to the Tozitna homesteaders that had met her at the ski strip. All except Stan's, as she handed him an armful of catalogs and letters she casually asked, "Is your team ready for Nome?"

Stan turned away facing his dogs. He took a slow analyzing look at Jumper, Sweeper, Maco, Louie, Lucky and Grizzly lying in harness along the side of the runway. After what could have been hours Stan slowly said, "Yep, we're ready."

"Great! because the entry fee is on its way." Claire blurted, unable to conceal her excitement.

Russ and Bill were close enough to catch the drift of the short conversation. They both grinned, thinking the same thing, "Here goes. Stan and Mike are over their heads once again."

Claire climbed back into her ski plane, as she leaned out to pull the door shut she yelled, " Stan, we'll see you in town soon as there's enough snow to cross the flats." Stan looked up from packing his sled and with a wide smile he nodded.

It was December 21. There was just over two months to get ready, not a lot of time for Stan to prepare for the thousand mile Iditarod race across Alaska.

We hadn't plan to cut it so tight, but my partner Claire

and I ran a low budget operation, we did not want to promise Stan the support if we couldn't come through.

I had spent the past week in Fairbanks finally able to swing a deal on a Cherokee Six. This plane would make the difference. I could supply Stan's team during training with the top meats while I hauled dog feed for the rest of the village to cover expenses. Then during the race we would fly support crew along the trail in case Stan wanted a new sled or needed to drop dogs. It all made good sense and sounded like a fun way to pass the winter.

For the past nine years Stan and Helen Zuray lived on their Tozitna homestead, forty miles due north of the village of Tanana. After driving their old Chevy from Boston, Stan and Helen literally started from scratch, and now had a beautiful place from where they fished, farmed and trapped. The Zurays lived the life many of us dream of, independent and free from civilized financial demands. They lived extremely well on very little.

I had known Stan three years. His high energy and enthusiasm was a definite bright spot on the river. The spring in his step made it appear that he rarely touched the ground. Short with a sinewy build, blond pony-tail and sparse beard, Stan rocked side to side during conversation as if he were about to run a foot race.

The previous winter we salvaged an old wrecked airplane off the tundra. Many laughed at my venture, all except Stàn. He volunteered his freight sled and powerful team to help haul the hudge Gullwing Stinson home.

While the tattered wreck sat perched on several sawhorses behind my cabin, Stan often joined me at the controls for make-believe journeys. My favorite was Stan mushing the Iditarod race with me flying support. We only took that fantasy ride once. Hoping not to wear out the dream potential, Stan nor I mentioned it again.

With Claire's help the old Stinson flew that summer.

A week after Claire had delivered the December mail, Stan and his team pulled into our yard. It was minus forty-five degrees and from his chewed up sled runners, obvious that there was little snow on the Tozi flats. This all made it clear Stan was excited about the race.

We stayed up late planning, how Stan would put training miles on his team, by running freight loads to the homesteaders on the Tozitna River, an eighty mile round trip. Stan needed more good dogs and planned to try out any canine offered.

Claire and I would help with the dog training as much as we could, but to cover the financial end we needed to work the Airplane hauling freight.

Word in the village traveled fast, we didn't need to advertise. Many enjoyed a good chuckle when they heard Stan was heading for Nome. He became the focus of long discussions. The population of dogs in Tanana was three times that of humans, no one from the area had yet competed in the race.

Stan's handling and care of his dogs was well appreciated by many in the village. Several offered Stan the pick of their large dog yards.

Early January the mercury stuck at minus fifty. With the extra training miles Stan was putting on his team, they needed a better diet. The spawned out salmon and rice just wasn't enough. The miles and cold temperature began to show in the team's performance.

I found a payload for the Cherokee to haul to Fairbanks. Claire had many hours in this aircraft type, she was to check me out under loaded conditions this first trip.

The ice fog set in soon after we landed and stayed thick for several days grounding us in Fairbanks. During this time we made contacts for various feed formulas, finally loading up the plane with eight hundred pounds of frozen ground liver, chicken and five gallon buckets of beef suet. There was barely room for our latest friend, Joe, a small solid husky pup one of the North Pole mushers had given us for Stan to try out.

Claire and I were anxious to get home and see how Stan's team would perform on this Super Premium race food mix. At noon the ice fog thinned, blue sky appeared through the haze. It took an hour of heating to start the large Cherokee engine. The ice fog had begun to settle back on the airfield, as daylight faded. With the inversion conditions we knew if we could climb up 200 feet the air temp was 40 degrees warmer.

Claire at the controls, the tires squeaked as we slowly rolled down the narrow taxiway. Phillips Field is narrow -even without the snow. When plowed, the snow berms on either side make it a real act to keep a low wing airplane centered, leaving several feet clearance on either side.

I cinched my seatbelt tight and turned to check the latch on the rear door. Joe lay flat on top of the large blocks of frozen meat, the brown patches around his eyes made it appear that he was smiling, excited about the trip.

 Claire pointed at the oil temperature gauge and nodded, it was time to head home. With the full load we used most of the short runway. Claire reached for another notch of flaps to help us break ground. I exhaled as the plane lifted frèe.

Then a quick hard jolt, the engine quit, we were thrown into the instrument panel as the plane stood on its nose plowing snow at eighty m.p.h.. Under the dim red lights of the cockpit we were locked into an eerie silence except for the hiss of dry snow over the airplane skin. The frozen block spilled forward squashing us into the panel. I was sure the plane would flip over. I looked up, with arms rigid against the dash, attempted to hold back the load. The plane settled right side up. I grabbed for the latch, we both crawled out. Claire was limping and doubled over holding her gut. She finally caught her breath and assured me she was OK.

A crew of mechanics ran out into the cold in various stages of dressing to help, with a rope and six men we were able to bring the tail down so the wreck didn't look so bad.

From the tracks it was clear the plane had drifted and caught a wing tip just after lift off. The prop and engine mount were bent, the nose gear tucked under the planes belly.

Now what?

I put off calling Tanana until late that evening. When I caught Stan overnighting at a friends, I broke the news .about our wreck, the phone line went silent....

"It looks like plan B now Stan, what ever that is," I tried to chuckle, "But the race is still on." I hoped to sound convincing.

Claire flew home, commercial, with as much dog feed as they let her take. I stayed in town to work on our new bent up Airplane.

Supporters rallied in the village, put on pancake feeds and a Mexican dinner to help raise money for Stan. Sandy Hamilton built a state of the art race sled he donated. Many of the women pitched in to sew dog booties, mitts and other gear needed for the race.

Nicknames have a way of suddenly appearing. Overnight Stan became Hip Hip Zuray.

Good feed was still a problem, not only expensive it cost alot to ship by air, my plan had fallen through.

It took three weeks of working outdoors under a tripod to get the Cherokee back in the air. After a nerve racking test flight from Fairbanks, Stan met me at the village runway with his freight sled, we unloaded the meat I had brought. As we each rode a runner into town I noticed his new team members, he informed me, "Yep I've run every dog on the river in the last three weeks. Nome here I come." It felt good to be home.

At the dinner table, Stan filled me in on his recent adventures of running other mushers' dogs. Assuring me he had his full team of eighteen members now, he went on about one big fluffy white samoyed-looking wheeldog he'd had only three days. "He's the best puller in the bunch, the owner told me he's neurotic and chews his feed cans to pieces."

"One thing I've noticed," Stan went on, "is it's usually the owner that has the problem and they lay it on the dog. That Dog just doesn't get enough running." Stan savvied dogs more than any one I knew so when he said he had a team ready for Nome that was that.

Outside his new team had been lying in harness still hitched to the sled. A few muffled yips, brought Stan to his feet and out the door.

When he returned, his dinner was cold. Ranting about that neurotic fluffy albino hound that was only good for his fur. Stan paced back and forth explaining what he had just found. The new dog had chewed himself free of the tow line. This was an acceptable offense for a new member, but then Stan noticed that several of the stanchions were loose and the brush bow was hanging off his sled.

After chewing free of the tow line, that hound had went on to chew and eat most of the caribou babiche that held the big freight sled together. This was a capital offense.

Stan ate his dinner standing up as I searched the cabin for any twine that might help to bind his sled back together for the forty mile trip to his homestead that evening.

The next several weeks we played catch up, Stan put the miles on his team, travelling the river, flats and in the timber. I stayed busy flying loads of feed.

One weekend we flew the cub over to visit Rick Swenson and Susan Butcher at Eureka hoping to pick up a few tips. I had met Rick through a dog swap the previous summer, he had invited me back, and now seemed like a prime time for a visit.

In two days we learned a lot, many time-saving tricks, like how to cook dogfood on the run, changing runners.

Training routines were shared by the handlers. I enjoyed watching as Stan worded a question in a round about way, Not wanting to appear to be prying, like one prospector asking another, "Was the gold high up or close to a river?"

After getting to know Stan, Susan with a big smile said, "I know You're no threat," then she cut loose with advice about trail strategy and necessities to carry in the sled. Swenson was in Fairbanks but his handler Marcus was more than willing to share all he had learned from Rick. We only wished he'd been around longer and knew more.

It was now February; time to get the thirty bags of trail food to Anchorage. Stan and I spent three days in Fairbanks thawing out his special menu to be mixed into paddies and divided among the various check points. Everything from ripe salmon liver to an old Grizzly bear that had eaten several of Stan's top dogs the previous summer, beaver, lamb, pork chops and pounds of butter for starters. All this mixed into fifteen hundred pounds of high-powered puppy burgers.

I headed for Anchorage with a truck load, Stan hopped a flight back to Tanana to pack up for the trip to the starting line in Anchorage. The new sled was finished, a new parka, mitts and assorted gear all came together at the last minute.

It took two plane loads to get Stan's team to Nenana, where we met Jon Huitt. His old lemon yellow International pickup had a new unpainted dog box mounted on its bed. Stan's race sled looked sharp on top with its brightly painted Hip Hip Zuray banner laced to the side rails. Each dog had a private berth while us three packed tightly into the narrow cab and aimed for Anchorage. We couldn't look any more professional.

There was only two days 'til Race time.

Driving through the night, the old truck almost did fifty mph. Out of a deep sleep I bolted upright to a loud bang. A tire blew, we swerved until Jon wrestled her to a stop inches from a steep enbankment.

As Jon jacked up the front, Stan mentioned how glad he was that the dog box was tightly secured. John stopped jacking and grinned. "I didn't have time to bolt it down Stan," he said. Stan dug out his tow line, within minutes the two layer dog box was crisscrossed with poly tugline.

Two days in Anchorage went fast, the banquet, meetings etc.. Then the Ceremonial Start at Kincaid Park. The long line of loaded dog trucks paraded out of the park climbing the steep Cordova Street hill. We were almost to the top when the line stopped, Jon pumped the brakes, the engine stalled, the old International started rolling backwards. In the wide side mirror, I could see the panicked face of the driver in the truck 50 ft. behind us. We picked up speed. Stan leaped onto John's lap to help stomp the brake pedal. I grabbed the door latch and made ready to jump.

I'd already been through one plane wreck and didn't feel it was my duty to ride this one out. As I yanked the handle we screeched to a stop within inches of ramming the brand new truck behind us. Jon gave Stan and I one of his wide-faced grins.

We ignored all the honking from the rear, finally the engine restarted. Ejecting a thick cloud of blue smoke with that burning clutch aroma we inched up the hill. I noticed the driver behind gave us lots of room from then on.

The official start scene was wild, 900 dogs all hyped to go, yapping, jumping and tugging at their lines. That is, all except Stan's team, they were layed out next to the truck, as if they were at the beach.

Comments like, " That team must be on drugs," was frequently heard from passing spectators. Even in the shoot

Stan's team laid down, which brought on a chuckle from the race officals. I rode the first six miles on top of the sled, jumping off at Knik check point.

We shook hands and I wished Stan the best. He mushed off fading among the snow weighted trees. I relaxed, Stan was in his Element, anything could happen now.

Weathered down in Tanana three days later, I caught the evening Iditarod update on the Anchorage news. They announced the first team was arriving into McGrath. The camera scanned the team, as they slid up to the check point. I cheered, it was Stan clear as day. He was several hours ahead of the pack looking well, the team stood wagging their tails.

Suddenly bets were changing in the village. The weather lifted, Claire and I were able to get to Ruby in her cub. Herbie Nyukpuk informed us, that Stan was having sled problems back on the trail. Claire and I waited anxiously into the night, at the edge of the village .

The temp was minus fifty, Stan arrived into Ruby at ten p.m.. The team looked great. Stan pointed to the sled and in disgust said, "This has cost me all my sleep time and slowed us to a halt." The sled had come apart, runners flattened out and delaminated, it was acting more like a scoop shovel.

We convinced Stan to sleep a couple hours, he agreed to three at the max. After spreading spruce bows for his team he crawled into a small cabin on the river bank. We pow-wowed at Mark Freshwater's cabin hoping to beg, borrow or steal another race sled.

Dr. Menniti had landed on the river earlier that day, he was returning a dismantled sled to Mark from Fairbanks. After twenty minutes of the locals scanning the village for a possible replacement, Mark offered to get tying his sled together for Stan. It took three pairs of hands tying three hours non-stop and the small sled was ready.

I woke Stan at three a.m.. He rubbed his eyes as he

approached the new sled, slid it back and forth, then jumped on and gave a kick. I ran along-side hoping to read his face as he glided in the dark. Stan rocked the small sled side to side then gave me a solid punch with a mitted hand and said, "I'm back in the race, Buddy."

He hitched up the team of sixteen they all gave one long howl. Stan pulled the ice hook free and glided out onto the snow-packed Yukon in the soft moonlight. That would be the last I'd get to see of Stan on the race, the weather came down which put a halt to our flying.

Traveling the river alone Stan made up time through Nulato, Kaltag and Old Women Pass.

Don Honea and team appeared in a blizzard forty miles west of Kaltag. He and Stan took turns breaking trail in the deep fresh snow, on into Unalakleet. At the checkpoint they were informed that the seven front runners were held up at Shagtoolik, unable to get across the ice to Koyuk. Don and Stan were now forty miles behind the leaders.

Stan knew this was the break he needed to catch up, but would he chance burning his team by pushing into the blizzard. He and Don rested several hours then decided to push on. After snacking the team, Stan chose Grizzly to lead into the wind. This would take the pressure off Jumper for awhile and save the amazing young leader for the final push into Nome.

The storm raged, sixty m.p.h. winds made it impossible for the lead dogs to hear the mushers commands. Grizzly was on her own to read the trail, Stan would stop the team often then walk up to encourage and praise his loyal friend.

After a long day on the trail they caught up with Swenson, Butcher and the other front runners in Shagtoolik. Now Stan hoped the storm would get worse so his team could rest while the competition was still pinned down in clear view.

Tanana was jumping. Stan was back up front. It was the only talk in town, bets were going down fast.

After thirty six hours the wind finally let up a bit. At first light, the nine teams well rested mushed out of Shagtoolik in single file onto the ice trail for Koyuk.

The pack travelled close together; Koyuk, Elim, Golovin, White Mountain. Dean Osmar had been holding the number one rookie position so far. Stan caught him just outside Golovin, they visited a few minutes then Stan and Don pulled ahead into White Mountain late that evening to take their mandatory four hour layover with the front racers.

After midnight all the teams left White Mountain within minutes of each other heading into Topkok, the last range of hills before the finish-line seventy miles west.

The wind increased on the hilltops causing a ground blizzard. When you looked straight up the stars were shining bright, but to look ahead the swirling, dry snow caused white-out conditions. Headlamps became a major concern, several of the mushers had new high-powered models with adjustable beams, but most had the dimmer version.

Don and Stan stopped their teams in along a slightly protected ridge for a short rest and snack. After twenty minutes they moved on. As Stan crested the next hill, he could barely see several headlamps fanned out in the valley below. It didn't look that bad from above but when he mushed on, it became obvious why the teams had spread out looking for the trail.

The valley caused a venturi-like affect, the wind increased building large drifts at random. Don and Stan walked ahead of their leaders trying to feel for the buried trail with their soft bottomed mukluks.

Conditions worsened through the night, the frustration of trying to catch up to the others with such poor visibility only made the hours seem like days.

At the bottom of the last hill before entering onto the Soloman Flats, a news crew and helicopter waited by the trail in the dark. The pilot told Don that the front seven racers had rested their two hours, then when they saw Don and Stans' dim headlamps coming down off the hill they all hurried and pushed on.

Two hours rest at this stage was too great of an advantage for the other teams to have, Stan knew that. But after nine hundred and fifty miles on the trail, the thought of trying to catch up once again tempted him. He walked over to his sprawled out team, they needed to rest after a hard night

Don gave Stan a warm punch and said with a big wind - burned smile. " Bud, we are in the Top Ten and you are the new Rookie of the Year, there's no one behind us for thirty miles, Relax."

Hearing Don, a respected race veteran confirm what Stan already knew deep down took the pressure off.

They enjoyed the next thirty miles. Don mushed down Front Street in eighth position, Stan was three minutes behind, and awarded Rookie of the Year.

Stan received a hero's reception on his return to Tanana.

It was right up there with the welcome that Lindberg got after his transatlantic flight, even the old fire truck started for Stan's parade.

Just Like Stan _____

Stan was our local Bush Guru.

He and his wife Helen had come north from Boston in 1970 to homestead in the Tozitna River Valley, forty miles north of the village of Tanana.

Don, their pilot, left Stan and Helen on a sandbar that sunny July day. He had already instructed them how to signal an aircraft when they had enough and wanted to return to civilization.

Over the years, Don had flown many greenhorns out into the Bush. He prided himself with his ability to closely estimate many of his passengers endurance and length of stay in the woods. Judging by Stan's small pile of supplies and tools, he gave the excited city couple until mid-September.

In their past ten years in the wilderness, they had done it all. They survived the early thin stretches on a diet of ravens. Then they cultivated the tundra and grew several acres of potatoes and other vegetables. The couple who were bet against turned out to be ingenious survivors, a resource for future settlers in the area.

Stan is short and sinewy with a blond ponytail. He walks with a bounce as though his heels are springs. Very few can keep up with him, besides his little wife, Helen.

If he doesn't find the parts he needs at the village dump, Stan builds it. He's substituted leather for gaskets, and often uses a hand file for many hours fabricating small precison pieces.

After a winter of chainsawing planks from extra large trees, planing and glueing, Stan pulled up to the town dock in a beautiful 24-foot riverboat.

There weren't enough salmon in the small Tozi River to supply Stan and Helen's growing dog team. He researched, then began his own hatchery by fertilizing and burying the eggs from the few fish caught in his nets. In three years, the salmon run on the river was enough to support several homesteaders and their many sled dogs.

All this was on an average income of three hundred dollars a year between them earned from Helen's birch baskets and Stan's small catch of fur.

It was no wonder newcomers to the Bush life search Stan and Helen out for tips on fishing, farming and just plain surviving in the tough environment of interior Alaska.

Lenny and Laurie planned to live on the Melozitna, the next valley west of the Tozitna. Motoring down the Yukon from Fairbanks in a big loaded riverboat, they decided to take a side trip up the Tozi to meet the famous Stan they'd heard so much about.

After securing their big boat in front of my house on the Yukon, they headed up the shallow Tozi in their canoe to visit Stan and Helen for a week.

They returned with many tips on homesteading and trapping. Then aimed for the mouth of the Melozitna farther down the Yukon.

The site Len and Laurie chose to build on was above a stretch of rapids on the Melozitna. This made it impossible to get their big boat and snowmachines up to the site. Everything had to be flown in by my wife, Claire, in her Supercub Bush plane.

I volunteered five hounds and dried salmon so they would have winter transportation if Lenny built a sled.

Claire, weighing in at ninety pounds, was the best payload pilot in Alaska. She could legally haul at least a hundred pounds more freight then most Bush pilots. Besides, she was superb at getting the plane in and out of tight strips most others wouldn't even attempt.

She hauled eight loads of Lenny's supplies in two days. As Claire taxied up for her second load the third day, I could see her wide grin even through the blowing dust and windshield.

"Okay, let's hear it," I said as I slid a fifty-pound bale of ripe salmon in behind the pilot's seat. She started, "I know I shouldn't laugh." Then she cracked up at the thought, and tried to continue, "Every time before I land, I circle their camp. Lenny runs out, jumps in his canoe and motors two bends down the river to the gravel bar I land on."

Claire went on explaining how Len stood up in the rear of the canoe, while the bow rode high above the water.

The last trip, Claire circled and landed, unloaded the Cub and waited, listening for the outboard hum signaling Lenny was just around the bend.

He never showed. After twenty minutes she climbed back in the plane and took off. She flew at tree-top level up the river to buzz the camp and let them know a load was waiting on the bar.

A canoe was floating midstream in the second bend. Claire's gut tightened at the sight of the empty boat. She scanned the glassy surface, praying Lenny had a life vest on.

A splashing on the river's edge was Len working his way along a sweeper that floated, it's roots still anchored to shore. Claire let out a sigh of relief as she banked the plane and headed for home.

The Melozi is a deep river; standing up to navigate didn't make sense. "Why was Lenny?" Claire cut in matter-of-factly. "Why else? He was doing it JUST LIKE STAN." She shrugged her shoulders and lifted a salmon bale. We both knew that Stan stood up in his flat-bottom boat to avoid riffles and boulders on the shallow Tozi. We had a chuckle thinking, Lenny's apprenticeship on the Tozi with Stan caused his dunking in the Melozi.

That was the beginning of the phrase "Just like Stan" that became as common as "Kilroy was Here" during the War. Many times newcomers would get in trouble imitating our Guru Stan.

Dave was the new preacher from Oklahoma. All he could talk about during spring races, was Stan's calm and obedient dog team. Dave went on, in his thick Okie drawl, about how Stan's dogs even laid down at the race gate, while the rest of the teams were going beserk. How they came in strong at the finish cause they save their energy.

"Soon my team is going to be like Stan's," Dave assured us.

There was very little snow left on the trail the evening Dave pulled his team up in front of our kitchen window. His voice could barely be heard as he walked among the team petting and talking to each pup. In the past you would have heard him hollering way before you ever saw a lead dog.

Finished with his pep talk, Dave knocked on the door, came in and invited Claire and me to a potluck at the church. Business concluded, he dipped a spoonful of honey into his tea, then sidestepped over to the window to check his team. They were all lying down. Dave relaxed, grabbed a chair and began a seminar on training sleddogs.

"They don't have to be wild and crazy. You just have to let 'em know you love em, by petting and talking to them.

Never need to raise your voice, neither. Then they'll be glad to wait for you. Just look out the window at mine. Now my dogs are just like Stan's team."

I turned my head and in a serious tone said, "What dogs?" Dave jumped up, spilling his tea. "Gone? They're gone?" His marten hat on sideways, he ran out the door yelling, "Jack, Jack, you no-good lead dog, I'll tan your hide." We could hear Dave for a quarter-mile. Claire and I were doubled over with laughter.

Dave had left his mitts on the table. He popped back in the door forty-five minutes later, after staking and tying his team to an old boat in the yard. He was afraid to leave them out of view for long. We worked up a concerned look.

Dave informed us his team had wrapped itself around a tree a half-mile downriver. "It's time now for advanced lessons." He chuckled, straightened his hat and was out the door. Last we saw, his team raced out of the yard as Dave waved a long willow branch and yelled homegrown obscenities from the runners.

When Stan mushed into town, I updated him on recent events caused by his influence. He would shake his head, smile and say, "That's not how I do it." Then he'd claim something must have been lost in the translation.

Results were not always mishaps, it was just that those stood out, adding to the village entertainment venue.

Everyone valued Stan's research and development skills. Most of us would sooner or later try one of Stan's approaches.

When Stan skimmed by on the Yukon one morning, his boat left a city-bus-like trail of fumes. I learned it was possible to mix diesel fuel and regular gas to run an outboard in a pinch.

Stan lived good, not knowing he was always in a pinch. To him it had only been progress since being left on the sandbar ten years ago.

That summer, Arman, a canoeist from Italy, pulled up to

our dock. I hired him for a week to help with a road-building project. He met Stan, who was in town putting up a cache of salmon.

Arman was intrigued by Stan and his Bush tales, especially how Stan, with only two month's preparation, had raced the Iditarod and won Rookie of the Year the previous winter.

Stan encouraged Arman to be the first from Italy to run the race. "It's a great way to see the country, meet people, and the dogs just follow the trail," Stan often said, reassuring Arman any time he expressed doubt.

At breakfast, following a late night bull session on the river bank, Arman informed us of his plans to return to Europe that fall, get a sponsor and race the Iditarod next spring. With a wide grin, Arman used his hands speaking Italian-English. "Maybe I win Rookie of the Year - just like Stan."

We were expecting it, but still the news was a mouthful.

I had some idea what it took to run the race. I had sponsored Stan and helped with details his first race.

With Arman out of earshot, I cornered Stan by the fish rack. "You better talk some sense into him, Stan. He thinks he's going on the race."

Stan smiled and nodded toward Arman, who was loading his canoe. Then he said, "With all that enthusiasm, he looks ready to me."

Arman finished his river trip and returned to Europe that October. I figured he was one more energetic foreigner we'd never see again.

That was until the Iditarod sign up list hit the Anchorage paper in December. There was Arman's name, plain as day.

Arman went on to run and complete two Iditarod races, then played a major role in getting the Alpinrod Race started in Europe. All along, doing exactly what he wanted - just like Stan.

Alaska still has its share of Stans. They help the rest of us push ourselves a little farther. Constantly they're a reminder that we already have so much more than we can buy. These few help keep Alaska wild and special.

Firewood on the River

The banks of the Yukon River are lined with huge drift logs, placed there by the high water of last spring's thaw.

A winter's worth of firewood can be a cinch using a boat and chainsaw. You motor upriver, cut the rootballs off, then roll the big logs into the water. Then you rope together a raft and let the current deliver your wood supply to town.

Many villagers wait until late September and moose season. They load the family into a flat-bottomed boat and head upriver thirty or forty miles. There they spend a couple of days assembling a raft while keeping an eye peeled for a fat bull moose. Then they drift home with their winter's cache of heat and protein.

Some rafts were like floating settlements - tents set up, meat drying on racks. Often the family sat around a campfire while the river carried them homeward at eight knots.

My first winter in the Bush, I almost froze, trying to heat a two-story cabin using a rusty old bow saw.

Now I was ready. A boat, chainsaw and company. Claire and Stan agreed to come along for the outing. Both had vested interest in this wood run.

Stan had spent many nights at my place the past winter. More than once he harnessed up his dog team in the middle of the night and headed for his homestead, forty miles north, saying it was warmer on the trail than in my living room.

Claire was considering spending the winter with me, but was more then concerned about the rumors she'd heard regarding the size of my woodpile.

We left at first light. The September sunrise illuminated the hillside of birch and cottonwood trees at their golden peaks. The river was mirror flat.

Twenty miles upriver, we pulled ashore next to a thick log jam piled high in a curve. Stan cut and trimmed while Claire and I rolled the big logs into the river using Can't Hooks.

They floated high in the water after a summer's drying in the sun. Most were already limbed and debarked from their rough trip among the Break-up ice the previous spring.

We lashed ten fat spruce together, then stacked six foot lengths on top in a sloped pile. This streamlined the raft for better control if the wind picked up.

By mid-afternoon, we had all the wood we could handle.

Stan and I shoved the raft into the current, then pulled the square bow of the boat against the butt ends of the long logs and tied on. Using the motor, we kept the raft in the main current.

The motor off, we all stretched out - feet up in the late afternoon sun, the raft drifted towards home. I never could have imagined that getting a supply of firewood could be so easy. A few hours work, then floating down a spectacular section of the Yukon River. This was hard to beat.

The evening chill had begun to set in as we drifted around 16 Mile curve and started down a long straight-away. I suggested setting the raft free. We could run home in the boat then meet the raft as it rounded Mission Hill curve two miles above the village.

If we timed it right we could tie on and encourage the raft to shore in front of the cabin. It sounded good to Stan and Claire. We rigged a flag on top of the raft for easier spotting and pushed free of the floating log pile. We planned to meet it in one hour at Mission curve.

Almost home, the outboard began sputtering. We barely made it to my dock.

While Stan and I worked on the engine, I constantly peered upriver, hoping the raft wouldn't show until we had enough power to push it ashore. I tried not to think about the many fishwheels that line the shore below the curve.

I knew well that if we didn't catch the raft in time, it would plow through the first fishwheel, and together they would wipe out everything in front of the village.

Finally the outboard would run, but only at three-quarter throttle, no lower. This sped the small boat along much faster then we needed.

Daylight was fading fast, Claire declined to accompany us as she handed me a box of battery head lamps and flashlights.

Stan shoved off; I aimed the bow upriver. Zipping along, we expected to find the raft just above Mission Hill curve. It wasn't there.

I was somewhat relieved, fiquring it must have slipped out of the main current and slowed down. I scanned with binoculars, but it was nowhere to be seen. The river along this stretch is less than a mile wide. We cut a zig-zagged route up the straight-away.

I knew we would come up on it soon.

Then we reached the place where we had set her free.

Stan looked back from his prone position in the bow and rolled his eyes back. It didn't make sense. How we could lose a six-cord wood raft on such a open straight-away?

We sped along, retracing our zig-zagged pattern. The big difference was now we were in pitch darkness, and several times the small tin boat skidded up onto the rocky beach. Stan and I jumped out and dragged the skiff thirty feet back into the water to continue our search.

The headlamps were useless. We both hung on with a white-knuckled grip.

As we zoomed along the river's surface into the pitch darkness, neither Stan nor I mentioned our greatest fear.

Thinking back how we stacked the raft, only one side had a slope to it. If we hit the slope at this speed we'd be launched airborne, boat and all. The other three sides of the raft would stop the boat, and launch Stan and me over the woodpile into the icy water.

None of this was very comforting.

If hitting it was the only way we could find the raft, I hoped for that flying sensation, while still attached to the boat.

Hope was thin. We were just around the curve from town and almost out of fuel. I knew the raft had beat us downriver and wiped out everything in its path. I became sick at the thought.

Whispering a short desperate prayer, I offered to do anything in trade for not having to replace every boat and fishwheel along the village riverbank.

The first aurora of the season began dancing high in the sky, silhouetting the hilltops along the river. I remembered an old Cree Indian who told me he could call the Northern Lights down by whistling. I began whistling as loud as I could.

Stan scooted back and aimed a dim flashlight into my face. Later he told me he'd thought I'd gone mad.

The rainbow of long shimmering ribbons slowly came closer and shone much brighter, now hovering well below the ridgetop. We were both mesmerized by nature's display.

Almost forgetting our chore.

Then I looked down. In the aurora's red reflection, the log raft floated directly in front of us.

I cut the throttle. We slid up along side the raft and tied on.

In seconds the Northern Lights vanished, and we were again in complete darkness.

Neither Stan or I mentioned a word.

Who would believe us.

McCann's Roadhouse located directly across from
the confluence of the Yukon and Tanana rivers, one
mile upriver from the village of Tanana.

Streisand, my first leader,

Richard, Fritz and wife Carla. Note one of the
'Flying Bacon Brothers' in the background.

After 29 years resting on her back, McCann
encourages Old *Blue* from the frozen tundra.

Old Blue one year later, sitting proudly at the
Tanana airfield.

"Let 'em Stick" Helen encouraging her team at the Tanana Spring Races.

Margaret O'Halloran, the *Irish Rose*.

Dr Jack Powers, Dir of Tanana Hospital
and Spring Dog race Marshall.

Stan Zuray at the starting gate of the 1982
Iditarod Sled Dog Race.

Stan's support team 600 miles down the trail at Ruby
- Lynda Johnson and Sherri, Zac, Seneca Runyan.

Chris and Bullwinkle

Stan in Nome after winning 'Rookie of the Year'
in the 1982 Iditarod. He kept the front running
veterans on their toes.

Michelle and Christopher
Homer, Alaska

Maxim, Pierre, and McCann returning from a
woodcutting trip along the Wabasca river.

Rich Ruggiero, back on th Hudson.
'Out for a Paddle'

Shanghai - the morning after.

Mike and Leah Ruggiero
'What Rabbit'

The author and his mother camped at the base of
Mount Washington in New Hampshire.

Chris, Michelle and Dad decked out with
Aunt Margaret on her Wedding Day.

THANKS, MOM
Kathleen Rudden McCann with a gift of roses from the
neighborhood gang.

River Rerun 1998.
The Powers family, Jack ,Viv, Taina and Jade revisit
the Yukon and village of Tanana with the Author and son Chris.

Stan Zuray, Charlie Campbell, Mike McCann, and Alex Tarnai on a clear crisp day in Tanana.

Part II

Flying in the
North Country

Flying Home the Bacon

Hoping to get legal, I flew my Cherokee Six into Fairbanks for a couple hours' flight instruction.

I needed freight to help with the gas back to the village, as this bird guzzled $40 worth an hour.

Early Friday morning I received a message to pick up eight hundred pounds of pork at McKee's, twenty-five miles north of town.

My freight was usually what other air carriers rejected: flammables, explosives. I couldn't understand why a load of meat was sent my way, until I pulled up to the farm.

This pork was still on the hoof.

Wrestling twenty hefty squealers into individual burlap sacks, I dreaded the twenty-five mile haul in the old station wagon, then an hour's flight to Tanana - this wasn't gonna be a high point in my life.

The chubbies packed tight in the wagon, radio blasting, muffler dragging, we headed for Fairbanks airport.

I needed two more hours of dual instruction to be signed off as a legal student. After one hour of crosswind landing practice, my instructor, Gary, informed me that he was unable to fly the second hour until possibly the next morning. His wife was three weeks overdue, the doctors were planning to induce labor shortly, and he needed to get to the hospital.

He suggested I stay the night and finish up tomorrow. I pointed to my old car, its windows fogged, rear bumper almost grounded, frowned and said I'd try.

Cruising around Fairbanks with my payload, it didn't take long to decide I had to get these grunting steamballs out of my life. Which could only mean load 'em up and fly'em out.

Backing the wagon up to the aircraft's rear cargo door, I proceeded to stuff four of these weiners into each of the dog kennels I had already secured on board. All this time I painfully admired my airplane's new plush velveteen Harlem Blue interior, which I had delayed installing until the winter sled-dog hauling season was over.

Now here I was, my first spring freight load, packing in the pungent porkers. I wouldn't have believed it if I'd been warned. The last two stinkers, I left stuffed in separate sacks and wedged both behind the pilot's seat.

While warming the engine I kept busy wiping the pig steam off the windshield with my wool cap.

Taxiing to the runway, my visibility was still limited. I frantically wiped the glass while speeding along, hoping to force fresh air into the vents and help clear out some of this toxic gas.

I knew from hauling dogs that once I got airborne, the inside fog would begin to clear.

Although, I was beginning to have my doubts.

"These pigs are definitely another kind of critter," I thought as I swerved down the taxiway. Headset on, radio full volume, I was barely able to make out the tower controller's clearance to TAKE OFF, over the squealing from the rear, which was painful even with my headset tight.

The take-off roll went fine until midway down the runway, when the plane bounced lightly off two waves in the tarmack. This forced my seat back and squeezed a sacked porker against a kennel. Once again, all hell broke loose. The kennels flexed at the seams as the oinkers writhed in a frenzy, like a load of netted salmon being hoisted on deck.

Thank God. The windshield began to clear as I lifted off and gained air speed.

One cure for my noisy passengers was less oxygen. I climbed to 12,000 feet. They all dozed off, grunting and snoring. Amen.

The stench had me holding my breath for most of an otherwise peaceful hour's flight across the tundra. I counted swans in the lakes on Minto Flats to avoid looking over my shoulder at the load of breathing bacon. Even as they tossed in their piggy dreams, they launched several subtle airborne reminders into my lap, in the form of turd chips.

Delaying descent until almost directly over the village gravel runway, I was hoping a short steep landing would be quieter than a gradual.

As my ears popped, so did theirs.

They all began screaming as if their tails had just been bitten off. I landed and taxied to the grass parking area, cutting the engine as I desperately sprang the door latch for air.

A small crowd surrounded the airplane, anxious to meet their new summer pets and winter cutlets. With a tinge of gleeful revenge, I opened the nearest kennel, freeing its four occupants into the grass, yelling, "Come and get 'em! Take your pick."

Most of these Indians had never seen a live pig, let alone catch one. It turned into more of a show than I had planned: twenty minutes of kids, pigs and adults running up and down the runway, finally exhausting all involved.

Cleaning off the remaining evidence from my once fancy Cherokee, I chuckled. I was thankful I didn't have a larger airplane: They could have been buffalo.

"I'm Not Lost - Where Are We?"

The Iditarod sled dog race was almost over. Butcher, Swenson and Joe May had just left Unalakeet sprinting their teams the final two hundred miles for Nome. The real race was on now.

Claire and I had been weathered down a week in the village of Tanana. The sky finally cleared. We loaded her PA-12 modified bush plane and planned to catch up with the front racers along the Seward Peninsula Trail, near White Mountain Village, 400 air miles west of Tanana.

Claire, a new friend, was also a commercial pilot. She flew daily for the local Native Corporation Air Service. This was to be our first long distance flight together. I was a student pilot, it was a relief to be flying with an experienced Alaskan bush pilot.

We lifted off Tanana's snow-packed runway on a cold and windy morning, the welcomed March sun shone brightly. The plane bucked a 25 mph headwind following the ice packed Yukon to Galena where we refueled and stashed three full five-gallon gas cans behind the passenger seat in case we needed to stop and add fuel to the wing tanks along the trail.

Claire had rigged her plane with wide skis that allowed her to land in deep powder snow.

After leaving Galena we followed the race trail to Kaltag. The village was bustling. We were tempted to land. Several race dog teams were pulling out onto the trail west of town. Claire circled then flew on, knowing if we stopped we could get held up, and not make the finish.

We followed the racers 40 miles into Old Women Pass then angled off over the Caribou Hills at a heading of 290 degrees N.W.. The country below was a washboard of snowcovered hills spotted with grazing caribou.

A strong side wind kept us crabbed-nose to the west. Claire and I passed the map back and forth many times, each pointing with a nod of agreement on our current location.

Beyond the hills, the Bering Sea appeared. Claire checked both wing fuel gauges then aimed the plane's nose over the sea ice, gliding   distance from shore.

My bladder told me we'd been flying a long time. Both gas tanks indicated less then one fourth full on the gauges.

A light haze covered the coast. We both confirmed that the bluff in the distance had to be Moses Point.

The sidewind turned into a headwind slowing our progress considerably.

Then the engine sputtered and quit!

Claire rocked the wings and switched the fuel lever. Restart wasn't immediate - the plane glided downward, the only sound being the loud hiss of air rushing over the wings. Land seemed a long way off.

Finally the engine roared to life lifting the nose high, I was forced back into the seat.

Bolt upright, Claire aligned with a narrow snogo trail at the water's edge while readying the plane to land.

The clatter of the metal skis on the hard packed trail never sounded so good.

We jumped out and refueled the wing tanks with the extra five gallon cans. Soon we'd be on our way up the coast to

Nome.

I sat on the right wing pouring gas into the chamois funnel. As I turned to reach for another can. I noticed two figures standing a half mile up the trail. They disappeared over a large snow berm.

Before I could mention them, we heard the zinging of snowmachine engines. They raced up the trail towards us.

Two older Eskimo gents wrapped in furry parkas and caribou mukluks dismounted from the snowgos. Each man shed a mitt. They came forward, hands outstretched offered a warm handshake. If it wasn't for the machinery I'd have thought we transcended a century.

Exchanging greetings, their English was broken. Their ear-to-ear smiles only grew wider when I said we were going to Nome and pointed up the coast.

"Kotzebue," the one said pointing down the trail behind Claire's plane.

"Koyuk," I said hoping I hadn't heard what I thought I heard.

"No, Kotzebue," he repeated.

Claire and I met eyes with serious questioning looks. She blurted, "I'm not lost!"

The other fellow pushed his parka hood back revealing a baseball cap with Kotzebue printed loud and clear across the front.

Claire shrugged her shoulders, mitts out, "But where are we?"

Each of us held a corner of the air chart down on the horizontal surface of the plane's tail, as we huddled to block the wind.

Sure enough we had missed Nome, by a longshot. About 45 degrees off course, then with the low lying haze we flew right past Kotzebue, a major village. We were well on our way to Point Hope thinking this coastline was the southern edge of the Seward Peninsula, with Nome just around the corner.

It would have been a long corner if we hadn't run low on fuel.

Invited for tea, we dragged up two drift logs and tied the airplane down. Claire and I shuffled up the narrow trail to the large snow berm where the two men had parked their snowgos. A tiny door was partially open, we ducked into the sodhut.

Two oil lamps on the table put out a soft light. It was very warm and cozy we felt we were at the northern most Hilton.

Still feeling very lost Claire repeated often, "I can't believe we could be so far off." It was gonna take a good while to sink in.

Tookruk with a serious look said, "I fly to Kotz with you." We both nodded glad to have him along.

It was almost dark when we swung the plane around and packed in. Twenty minutes to Kotzebue went fast. The haze was thick around the airport. The skis squeaked on the dry snow as Claire taxied to the transient parking area. The temperature was minus forty and dropping fast. After tying down we followed Tookruk through the village to his brother Ken's. It was a large house by artic standards, full of kids. The action stopped as we unwrapped in the living room, Tookruk explained our plight in Eskimo.

The smiles enlarged. We shook hands and sat down to the busy table and ate juicy reindeer steaks. After hearing details of our story Ken disappeared, an hour later he returned his Parka covered with frost. He kicked the snow off his caribou mukluks in the porch way. Then walked towards Claire, in his large mitted hand was a small blackfrosted instrument.

"You can mail this back to me when you get home to Tanana, I know it works," he said as he carefully placed the small compass in Claire's cupped hands.

Ken had just spent the previous hour outside at the airport

extracting the instrument from his airplane.

Claire looked across the table at me, she was stunned, slightly shaking her head in disbelief.

Late that evening, we hiked out to the plane to light the propane asbestos heater that would allow us an early departure. On the way, Claire mentioned Ken's loaning her his compass. She still couldn't believe the warmth and hospitality shone by this Eskimo family to total strangers.

Early the next morning we bid farewell to our new friends wishing we could stay longer.

We kept the map out and followed the trail to Candle. A good stiff tailwind encouraged our flying, visibility was clear. Mountain Village, 70 miles from Nome, appeared on the hill. We circled and landed to find out where the front racer might be.

As the prop stopped we slid to a halt, I lifted the plexiglass door. A short bundled up man with many cameras hanging from his neck ran up to the plane. In a thick German accent he loudly explained, "I am lost! I come from Berlin to write a book about the race, now I miss the finish, you must help me."

"Lost, how could you get lost out here? There is only one trail." He understood and didn't appreciate my humor.

The front mushers had left the village several hours ago. We enjoyed coffee with an older Eskimo couple manning the check station. Then packed our new friend, Wilhelm, into the cub. We flew the race trail catching up to Joe May, Swenson and Butcher, who were battling for first place.

Wilhelm's camera clicked away. Claire landed on the ice so he could get more action photographs, as the teams mushed into Safety, the last check station before Nome.

Joe May won the race that year.

Over a large pizza we explained to Wilhelm how we had gotten lost and traveled 300 miles off course just the day before. He obviously enjoyed the story.

"You don't have to include that in your book," I almost pleaded.

Two Days with Blackie ____

The bears had been raising hell with us that summer. Last week a large black chased my wife, Claire, and her fish-cutting partner, Linda, up the fish-drying rack. Claire was able to ready her Dad's old 30.06 and, with one tonsil shot, put him on the barbeque grill.

I tolerated them knocking over the salmon racks, eating the seats off our old sno-goes, munching on the rawhide that held the dogs sleds together. But scaring me back into the outhouse daily was getting old.

A houseful of European guests made me late for a twenty-five mile freight run up the Yukon River. I'd promised two Danish friends, Hans and Fleming, I'd meet them at dark on the beach below the mine with building materials for their new cabin.

The full September moon glared over the ridge.

I preferred river travel under the moonlight; it was usually calm and extra peaceful on the water. I hustled to get the boat loaded and be on my way.

Bidding farewell to the houseguests, I promised Blackie and Anna, our latest arrivals from Germany, that I'd be back in time for their scheduled flight the next morning.

Blackie had spent the previous winter trapping with Russ

and Stan, homesteaders in the Tozitna Valley. He then returned to Germany, retrieved his girlfriend, Anna, and now planned to give her a tour of his winter stomping grounds.

Previously I asked Blackie the origin of his name. He informed me it was given to him, because he was tall, dark and handsome.

Shouldering my rifle strap, I pulled the kitchen door closed behind me, stepping onto the enclosed porch. Then I bent down, grabbed two five-gallon gas cans and butted the outer door open with my head.

The door instantly ricocheted, forcefully flattening my nose. Stunned and trying to focus, I could make out a large black furball heading north. I stormed back into the house, interrupted the group discussion, yelling, "Blackie, here's your bear!"

I handed him my rifle and pointed down the soggy narrow trail. Blackie departed with five of us river rats on his heels.

A quarter-mile into the thick, he suddenly crouched and aimed his rifle high into a spruce tree. Scrunching his eyebrows in a severely confused look, he whispered in his thick German accent.

"Bear has no gott dam' body!"

"Don't shoot! Don't shoot! Blackie, that's the bear that chased Claire on the beach last week. The rest of him is in the smokehouse. Yours is long gone."

"What the hell his head is up in the tree for?"

"To save it I put it up high so the birds would pick it clean."

Everyone else was in hysterics as I tried consoling Blackie, promising there'd be another bear during his three-week visit. He muttered under his breath in German.

The river run went well. Hans and Fleming had a bonfire going on the beach when I pulled in. We off-loaded the plywood, two-by-fours and roofing tin, then packed it up the bank to the thick brush, so they could shuttle it back the mile into the cabin site.

A long night was spent on the beach by the fire. At 3 a.m. a storm moved in, the wind white-capping the river, and a light snow covering the ground. Even with an early start, my return was delayed by the rough water.

I pulled into our dock early afternoon, still having daylight to fly Blackie and Anna over the Tozitna River Valley.

I'd agreed earlier to give them a tour, but did not want to land on any lakes. In the fall, just before freeze-up, the lakes are often shallow and thick with floating moss, a dangerous combination for landing a floatplane.

While readying the Super Cub, I heard a German dialogue and turned to see Blackie and Anna packing a week's gear down the riverbank trail to the dock.

"You need all your gear for a one hour's scenic flight?" I shouted, perturbed.

Blackie whined, "Please, Mike, it's been raining lots. I know Stan's Lake is safe. You can drop us off there."

Well, I knew I'd have a better chance at talking Mother Liberty into putting her arm down than reasoning with Blackie.

"OK, let's load up, but any moss showing, I'm not landing."

Packed tightly in the small Piper Cruiser, we bobbed and splashed out into the main current. I turned into the upriver wind and gave her full power. With the ten mile an hour current and thirty mph headwind, we broke loose on the third wave crest.

Climbing, I banked the plane north, and skirted snow squalls and mountain tops to get over the pass to the Tozitna River.

Descending into the valley flats, we zig-zagged at three hundred feet, scouted for the trail or landmarks. Finally making out the Tozi River, I flew a large circle to the northeast, hoping to see Stan's Lake.

The snow got thicker. I was about to cancel when I caught

view of the lake just off my right wing tip. Circling several times, I could make out a large open path free of moss, a space in which I hoped I could set down and get stopped.

Blackie just about perched on my shoulder, repeating, "Looks good, looks very good," until I hollered.

"Who the hell is flying this crate? If I'm gonna screw up this landing, I don't want you talking me into it. I want full credit."

Approach and touchdown went smoothly. Then a side gust pushed us off the clear way into the moss. The plane stopped fifty feet from shore; using power would only cover the wings and control cables with a thin layer of ice, and still might not get us in.

I'd have to climb out and turn us around manually, then fire up and taxi for an open shot at the shore.

Cutting the engine, I climbed out onto the floats, telling Blackie, "Sit tight." Then I donned my hip boots, and untied two canoe paddles from the float struts.

The paddles laid flat on the moss under the plane. I used them like snowshoes to keep me from sinking in the moss while I rocked and pushed the airplane backward into the open water.

After several minutes of serious effort and little headway, I stopped for a breather, looked up to see Blackie balancing at the front of the right float with nothing on but his Fruit of the Looms. I shouted, "This stuff is bottomless Blackie, will ya cool your heels?" No use. Off he leaps into the frigid Alaskan water, sinking to his waist.

He stood in the lake, with a minor voice pitch change clapped his hands and gave instructions in German to Anna.

The plane was moved easier minus his two hundred pounds. I encouraged him to crawl for shore since he was turning blue and shaking violently while trying to assist me.

Oh', no. I could not believe my eyes. From my angle they

looked like a pair of chalk sticks with pink panties on.

Anna was climbing out of the cockpit onto the float almost completely dethreaded. Before I could interrupt Blackie's instructions, she leaped high onto his back, driving him up to his earlobes in the endless muck. Anna scampered up onto his shoulders, trying not to get wet.

Blackie screamed, "Nein Dumkopf," over and over at the top of his lungs.

I helped Anna back onto the float.

It took a lot of pulling, twisting and prying with a paddle to free Blackie from the muck.

I was very concerned. I'd never seen a human being the color of a blueberry. His lips quivered so fast and hard, he couldn't speak. I must admit, I was grateful for that.

Meanwhile the plane, slid back, freed itself of the moss. We all climbed in. I fired up the engine and taxied around to an opening for shore.

Their gear unloaded, we lit up a survival stove for tea as they dressed, muttering all along in German.

Trying to keep Blackie from sitting on the stoveburner, I drew a map to Stan's vacant homestead, where they could spend the night.

Shaking hands, I promised them I'd look for them in a week if they didn't make it back to our village.

After take-off, I banked the plane steep to the right and buzzed them at twenty feet as they started their trek across the tundra.

Blackie and Anna both had big wide grins. They waved vigorously. I rocked my wing tips in farewell and headed home.

I chuckled, thinking to myself, "Two days with Blackie! I'd forgotten how much fun he can be."

104 ❖ Give Me the Hudson or the Yukon

Tail Heavy _____

Noreen liked to eat.

Her last year in the village, she gained a hundred pounds, pegging the hospital freight scale at four-twenty-five. How Knute fit her into his little Stinson airplane is still a mystery. The fact that they lifted off the short gravel airstrip at all defied the laws of gravity and aerodynamics.

It was late on an October day and snowing lightly: not a good time for a hundred-fifty-mile flight across the tundra to the village of Nenana. First word the next morning was that Knute and Noreen had never arrived at their destination. It was search time. Thirty planes from all directions converged, scanning and criss-crossing Knute's probable flight path.

The temperature hadn't risen above zero and a light snow persisted. Poor conditions in which to be looking for a small white airplane. The first day was fruitless. That evening, with their planes bedded down, the searchers gathered in town around woodstoves drinking tea and speculating.

Did Knute follow the wrong drainage? Was it weather? Did Knute's compass work? No, all agreed. Knute had been in the country too long for those mistakes. He knew the rivers and country like a wolverine. So what could've happened?

Thinking of Noreen packed into that tiny airplane, all were

concerned, hoping Knute hadn't had to put down hard. If
he had, I could only pray her seat belt had held, otherwise
she could've driven Knute through the instrument panel as
though it were a cheese grater. It was best not to dwell on
details.

In the past, Knute had often said with a wide grin, "I hate
chopping wood. I would much rather buy groceries to heat
the cabin." And since he and Noreen had moved into their
little cabin in the center of the village, barely a wood pile
ever existed at their doorstep. Between Noreen's love for baking
pies, and her rather large radiant surface area, they had survived
two severe winters comfortably.

At the break of dawn, all searchers were airborne. The
new plan was to fan out and broaden the search path to a
width of fifty miles, in case a strong side wind had exhausted
Knute's fuel, forcing him down, hopefully on a sandbar or
in a clearing. The bright sun helped a bit, only now the country
was covered with a thick blanket of fresh snow. Since Knute
was known for his limited survival gear - at the most, a ball
of bailing twine and a candy bar - we all knew if he and
Noreen had crashed, today had to be the day they were found.

The pilots agreed to get down low - 200 feet - and fly
a tighter grid pattern. It would be the only way to see Knute's
plane in the fresh snow. Spotters and pilots spent a long morning
criss-crossing the tundra. The sun helped, but strained eyes,
and by midday was wearing on all who peered down, not
wanting to miss a square foot. The pilots flew carefully to
avoid each other. Radio communications tied up three chan-
nels, and as daylight passed by, voices changed pitch to one
of concerned tension.

Two p.m., Danny Hotchkiss heading to the Nenana runway
for refueling. Fifteen miles out, his spotter tapped his shoulder,
hollering "Circle left!" Joe swore he saw two numbers on a
snow patch forty-five degrees down below their left wing.

Banking the plane, it became obvious that Knute's Stinson was nose first into a thicket of scrawny black spruce. Flying a tighter circle, they could make out Knute under the right wing of the wreck, wrapped in a dull red engine cover, attempting to get up and waving furiously. Noreen waved, shaking the Stinson, which released a puff of snow from several spruce trees.

Danny breathed a deep sigh of relief. Knute and Noreen were his close friends, and only then did he realize how tense he'd been, worrying about them. He sat high in the seat, firewalling the throttle while his spotter, Joe, plotted the site on the map. Within thirty minutes, there was a military chopper from Fairbanks lowering a rescue net to the wreck.

Knute's version of the events from his hospital bed was that when the snow got thicker, he'd considered landing on a survey line. Suddenly he was in a whiteout. Relying on his limited instrument panel, he tried to keep the wings level and slowly gain altitude. Then trees appeared and began tugging on the landing gear. A loud whack and a jerk brought the plane down.

When Knute came to, all was quiet. His left side felt as if a polar bear had clamped on, blood reminded him more of thick mayonnaise as he pressed the wound. His sternum was stiff from bouncing off the control yoke. "Thank God for seat belts," he prayed with shallow breath.

He reached behind the seat with both hands - she was gone! "Noreen!" He tried to yell. "Noreen!"

"I'm OK, Knute." Her voice came from off to the right. "I'm trying to stand up in this mucky crap. Are you all right, Knute?"

"Shit, I'm pinned and bleeding a little," he said softly.

The engine mount tubing had come through the firewall on the left side, locking his hip against the seat. The pain had blacked him out. Any movement now hurt like hell.

Noreen crawled toward the wreck, attempting to stand with the aid of the bigger spruce. She would get two-thirds up, waver, and Snap! She and half a fire-hardened tree would bounce onto the tussocks.

"The wing," she thought. She could barely make out its Hershey bar shape suspended off the ground twenty feet away. Kneeling below the wing tip, she reached up to grab the aileron hanger and NAV light for assistance. As she pulled, the plane rocked. Knute screamed in agony. She let go, falling backward.

"Please don't rock the plane," he begged. He grabbed around in the cockpit for anything to wrap in - his coveralls just weren't enough. "Noreen, I'm freezing. Please try and get to the baggage door." He'd almost froze before and knew he'd better get covered before the euphoria stage set in. Noreen was doing her best, working along the wing. She grabbed at anything and everything. Snap. Boom. Knute couldn't believe his ears. In the dark she sounded like a moose in rut. Finally crawling up to the fuselage on her knees, she was able to open the rear baggage compartment and slide out the old oily, torn engine cover.

Knute wrapped himself in it, teeth chattering. Noreen, in a big parka and Sorel felt-lined boots, didn't feel cold at all. Both passed out from exhaustion, Knute pinned in the front seat, Noreen under the right wing.

After a long, painful night, Knute was ready for a change. Gathering all his strength in his gorilla-like torso, he was able to force the mount tubing several inches out of his lap, allowing him to slide to the right. The relief was overwhelming, until he looked down and saw that his hip ball was completely dislocated, as if he had a cueball in his left pocket. The sight weakened him.

Again bracing himself against the pain, he was able to lower himself from the Stinson on one leg. He got around better than Noreen. Using a quart of motor oil and branches, he was able to get a small fire started. They huddled together under the greasy engine cover. He was sure glad now that he'd brought a big woman along.

As they hovered fifty feet over the wreck site, the rescue team couldn't believe their eyes. Knute was helping Noreen into the net first. The GI on the hoist control hollered into the copter intercom, "This is a test!"

The rescue went well. Knute and Noreen rested in the Fairbanks Hospital several days.

Noreen got a stomach staple job for Christmas. She lost 180 pounds in six months. Knute's cutting a bit more wood these days. His new plane flies higher and glides a lot farther.

Hanging High

Every evening for the past two weeks, we practiced - arching, landing rolls, emergencies, and folding the old Army para- chutes. The students were ready for their first jump.

Saturday morning was cool and calm, perfect for initiating new skydivers. The hangar buzzed. Twenty students and five instructors, several lunging off a shaky old work bench practicing tucks and rolls. A few spent quiet moments, off to the side, wondering.

The Cessna 182 warmed up outside on the ramp. I checked the manifest sheet tacked up on the wall. Four students, with me as jumpmaster, were on the first flight. I called the names. Brian and Roxanne leaped through the doorway, while Jeff and Mahoney slowly shuffled forward.

Each jumper's helmet and chute pack checked, I then positioned the students tightly on the floor of the aircraft. The rear door and all of the seats, except the pilot's, had been removed to help make it safer and easier to exit in the air.

I squeezed in last, behind Mahoney. He was to go out first. He'd never been in a small aircraft. I didn't want to give him too much time to think about it. He already looked a mild shade of avocado green, and we hadn't left the ground.

I gave the thumbs-up sign to Dave the pilot, a big, good-natured, balding ex-war pilot. Dave always had a wide smile and would fly all day hauling jumpers if needed.

Take off and climb out were standard. When the large orange Xs spread out in the center of the jump zone were directly underneath, I pointed down. All four heads nodded in slow motion.

Each student's ripcord was hooked to a thirty-foot static line, which was secured to the aircraft. As each person jumped and was thirty feet clear of the plane, the chute would automatically open. The rules were that every student made five static line jumps before free-falling, giving them time to develop skills and avoid panic and possible freeze-up.

I held up my arm so everyone could see the large altimeter strapped to my wrist. Mahoney was to go out at 2700 feet. We were nearing 2500. I tapped Mahoney twice on the shoulder - the get-ready signal. He pivoted, swung both legs out into the 80 mph slip-stream and extended his left leg for the small step. He turned his head quick. Close to my face, he hollered, "Slow the damn plane down!"

He was stalling. "We can't go any slower. Go ahead!" I thumped him twice again. "You know what you have to do: swing out, grab the wing strut, then arch."

"I'll hit that tail!" he shouted back. Then he tried to reach behind him and pull his way back into the group.

"Mahoney!" I screamed.

Suddenly he spun toward the edge. He reached backward, pointing both hands over his helmet like a diver, and launched himself from the tiny step with a blood-curdling scream, as if from the high board.

I'd never seen that style before.

When the plane quit rocking, I was able to look down and see his full canopy open. I breathed a sigh of relief for Mahoney. The other students went out with no problem. I was glad Mahoney's demonstration didn't rub off on anyone else.

Dave kept the plane climbing. We'd agreed earlier that I'd go out at 8500 feet for a long relaxing free-fall. Rocking the wings to get my attention, he put his hands overhead, in Mahoney's jumping stance and smiled. I could only shrug my shoulders.

"Anything is possible when someone gets excited," I thought. "And he was convinced he was gonna hit the tail - a fear I need to mention in ground class."

Dave gave me the high sign and leveled off. It was my turn. I planned to free-fall to 3000 feet. I swung out, grabbed the strut, arched and released.

A sudden hard jerk. My left leg hurt like hell. I was facing up, and knew I was in trouble.

A static line had tangled around my ankle. I was dragging twenty-five feet behind the airplane, which was descending in a tight spiral. I was flapping around like a kite tail. I tried to reach the cord.

I grabbed my left thigh with both hands. The drag was too much. I couldn't flex forward, I couldn't release myself.

The other end of the static line was hooked to the base of Dave's seat. I kicked and twisted like a fish on a hook, jerking as hard as I could, and praying Dave would feel me dangling behind. He didn't.

I prayed fast and hard, "Please, someone on the ground or in the tower, try the radio." But I knew Dave rarely used his radio.

I dug a Swiss army knife from my pocket, exhaled and flexed forward hard, reaching for the strap with the shiny blade. The heavy woven line evaded my attempts by inches.

My altimeter read 4500 feet.

I had a decision to make. It wasn't an easy one. I knew I couldn't survive being dragged down the runway at eighty miles an hour. If I pulled my rip cord, the chute would open. If the force didn't snap the static line, my leg would have to give.

At that thought, I almost vomited. Still, my chance of surviving was better. It took a few seconds to absorb this fact.

We were at 2800 feet now. I was becoming disoriented from whipping around behind the diving airplane. Closing my eyes, I grabbed the cold steel ripcord ring, clenched my teeth, arched back and pulled.

The pain knocked me out. For how long, I wasn't sure.

When I could focus again, my whole body was numb. Looking up, I saw the canopy in full bloom. I crouched in my harness, afraid to look down.

The ground was getting close. From my waist down, I couldn't feel a thing.

"I'd better see what I have left to land with," I thought. I could see both knees in clear view. I breathed again.

Leaning forward in my harness, I saw what I couldn't feel: my left foot. I was still intact.

Sagging in relief, I thought, "The line snapped. Thank God for these old military surplus goods." Then I felt a tugging as my leg awakened.

Looking down the thirty-foot woven line, I couldn't believe my eyes. There was the pilot's seat, dangling empty.

It took Dave forty-five minutes to land the airplane without a seat.

Dave later explained that when the seat disappeared from underneath him, he fell backwards, sending the plane into a loop. He fought hard to get back to the controls and not be thrown out the open side door of the thrashing craft.

Finally at the controls again, it was still no easy chore to land while sitting on the floor.

That's why the numerous approaches, with only the top of a bobbing head visible at the window, until the fuel ran dry. Then a very decent landing, considering.

Dave stood with his large farm-worn hand on my shoulder

as I stared into the seatless plane parked in front of the hangar. "Sure am glad my seatbelt wasn't bolted to that bent-up seat," he said in a serious tone, as he pointed to the culprit seat lying on the ground.

I nodded, envisoning Dave strapped into the dangling seat thirty feet below me as I descended on that last jump.

Then with a slow grin, he said, "And please, please don't hook any more static lines to my seat." I teetered on my now slightly longer leg, "Not a chance, Dave."

Note: Mostly true. That's what the title promised. And this is the only story in the collection that's not right on the money- only because the author wrote it in the first person to make it easier to tell. It really happened, and Mike McCann was there. He was actually Mahoney, the freestyle jumper.

Old Blue

A cool, clear June morning saw Old Blue and me lift off from Fairbanks Metro Airfield for her last time, packed with a good-sized load, including spare engine parts, tools, survival gear and a rocking chair. I had to search for the pilot's seat.

After a smooth engine run up, I aimed down the narrow airstrip and pushed in full power. Within yards, her tail was up. We sprang along on the main gear, over the wavy tarmack, then with a leap, the thick, gull-shaped wings pulled her skyward.

Climbing, she sounded like a D-8 Cat pulling a sled load up a steep hill, but once at 8,000 feet altitude, prop and engine slowed down to eighteen inches and 1800 rpms. Old Blue purred and flew like the beautiful, new Gullwing Stinson she'd been back in '36.

Following the Tanana River east, we had a good stiff tail wind. In two hours we were closing in on the Canadian border. I was not digesting this fact well. As the tail wind died off, Old Blue slowed down, seeming to hesitate herself.

She had been in Alaska since '49 except for four months in '81 when my friend Claire and I hauled her to Montana to recover her. Thirty of those years, she had lain on her back in the tundra, slowly settling into the ice and tussocks. Many a cold trapper found shelter in her tattered cabin, often stripping a piece of wing rib or engine hose to repair a faulty snow machine or patch a broken dog sled.

From the air, she was a landmark: this big yellow fuselage among the short black spruce. She was well known among the Yukon River Bush pilots, alerting them that they were fifteen miles west of the village of Tanana.

Now, about to cross the north-south survey line that indicates the official U.S.-Canada boundary, I banked into a shallow left turn, flying two large circles. The action seemed to be slowed down. My mind was racing.

Hard to believe I was leaving Alaska, even harder to conceive that Old Blue would probably never return, bound for sale to a collector in the Lower Forty-Eight.

Leveling off, I rocked the wings in salute to a great state, took a deep breath and crossed the border as if it were the Iron Curtain. I knew the route well and planned to fly along the Alcan Highway. In case of severe weather or mechanical problems, I could set her down, hopefully with little damage.

There was lots to think about on this trip. Often I tried to imagine what it was like for Joe Cook, who had parked the Stinson on the tundra in the fall of '52.

Joe spent a rough three days trying to fly to Fairbanks from Galena, a small village in western Alaska. The first day, due to icing and poor visibility, he was forced to land on a sandbar along the Tanana River. After spending the night sleeping wrapped in a grimy sleeping bag in the cockpit, he was able to take off the next morning. He flew low over the countryside, hoping to find a cloud break that would allow him to make it into Nenana. Heavy icing forced Joe instead onto a hillside in the Redlands area forty miles north of Nenana.

Using a small hatchet, Joe spent the afternoon clearing a path across the slope through the black spruce for a possible runway. Temperatures had dropped, and by the time Joe was ready to attempt a take-off on his airstrip, the engine oil had thickened enough that the battery couldn't turn the propeller fast enough to get cranking. Engine heat was needed.

Joe jumped from the cockpit, grabbed armfuls of brush, stacked it under the engine cowl. Running short on daylight encouraged Joe to drain several gallons of AV gas from the tank and pour it on the brush pile. In a puff, the nose of the Stinson was engulfed in flames. Dense, black smoke billowed out from under the old sleeping bag he had also used as an engine cowl cover.

In a frenzy, dancing a high-speed Irish jig, Joe was able to kick the blazing brush away from the airplane. Then, wrapping the bag completely around the engine cowl, he begged in desperation, "Please Don't Blow." knowing well if the carburetor gas caught, it would be curtains for this airplane. The fire smothered. He lay back against the windshield. The plane was saved, but what next?

The snow was getting heavier and it was almost dark. Joe crawled into the cockpit, wrapped up in the burned sleeping bag that had just saved his only way out of - wherever - and slept.

Awake before light and knowing today had to be it, as he had only two candy bars and a half a container of water, Joe planned his approach. Heat the oil and engine separately. Fumbling around in the dark, he built a fire, well away from the aircraft. Joe drained the engine oil into a five-gallon pail, then hung it over the fire. Next, he built a small fire under the plane's nose, needing to heat the massive radial engine case, for pouring warm oil into it would be futile. As light crept over the horizon, Joe could see the clouds had lifted. If he could just get in the air and aim north, he knew he would intercept the Yukon River.

Two hours later, the bucket of oil was plenty hot, the engine case warm to the touch. Joe tossed the ratty engine cover aside as he climbed up to pour the five gallons of hot oil into the reservoir tank, hoping some of the heat would help defrost the windshield, too. He knew he would need all the visibility he could get to maneuver down his narrow, slanted, homemade runway. He stamped out both fires, leaped in and pumped the primer knob five solid strokes, kicking down hard on the starter button. She roared to life; no uneven popping. Hard to believe the electrical harness had survived the previous night's torching.

A steady sixty pounds of oil pressure registered on the gauge. Clenching his teeth, he grunted a short prayer and gave her full power. The plane waddled a bit; the tail wheel was hung up in the short brush. Joe worked the yoke back and forth until the tail sprang up and released. The propeller sucked snow, ashes and small twigs past the howling bird. She started rolling while sliding sideways down the slope. Soon the left wingtip was in the trees. Cutting the engine to idle, Joe jumped out, flailing his axe, clearing more trees, then pushing the tail sideways. Several more such delays and Joe was at the far end of his new airfield.

Turning her around was no easy chore. Finally aiming back down the runway, he hoped the engine torque would help him keep the plane out of the downhill brush. Full power again. Slow start, but gaining speed. She lifted off.

Joe banked her over the flats, heading north for the Yukon River. It took full power to keep her flying, due to the previous semi-crash landings which removed most of the lower side fabric and much of the tail's covering. In thirty minutes he could see the Yukon, but both gas gauges indicated below empty.

"She'll make it."

He had just completed this thought when the engine began sputtering. Then all was so quiet, he could hear the air hissing over those big wings.

"Shit!"

Rocking the wings, Joe hoped for an extra cup of fuel, as he searched for another place to crash land. He said later, "I thought she'd glide to the river, but all torn up - she came down like a streamlined rock."

Again onto the tundra she bounced and lurched, then flipped hard, ejecting Joe through the front windshield into the semi-frozen muck. He was okay, but getting tired of the trip.

His big yellow airplane looked bad. The worst he'd ever seen her. Lying on her back, small spruce trees sticking clear through her wings. Wheels ten feet in the air. Shaking his head as he turned, he felt as if he was leaving an old pal at the graveyard, six feet under. He couldn't believe she was finished.

He grabbed his gun and greasy bag, took one last look, and hiked three miles to the Yukon River, then trudged fifteen miles to a sand-spit across from the village of Tanana. To get attention, he fired two shotgun blasts, then lay down in the snow, exhausted. A Federal Aviation Administration mechanic heard the shots, flew a small J-3 over and picked up one hungry, worn-out Joe Cook.

Old Blue and I crossed Lake Kluane with a forty mph headwind, then turned east at Haines Junction. When Claire and I had flown Blue home from Montana over this route in '81, the old bird flew double time, as if going back to Alaska had supercharged her, like a horse heading for the barn. Although she was indicating 115 mph, all calculations gave us 145 mph groundspeed. Now I was flying 80 mph, hoping I wouldn't run short on fuel and have to pick an alternate airstrip. I could only think Blue wasn't anxious to meet the customs man in Whitehorse.

As we rounded the last bend of the Mendenhall River, Whitehorse Airport came into view. Not rocking the wings, I did a straight and level turn, lined up and landed, taxiing over to the FSS where a small crowd of mechanics gathered under Blue's wings. Several of them remembered her from our flight north in '81. That evening, rolled up under the midnight sun in the deep grass, I thought of how fortunate I was to own such a beautiful old plane, and of the unusual circumstances which had led to this flight.

I had come to Alaska to learn to fly. After two years of working as a nurse in a small Bush hospital in Tanana, I took my bankroll of $4,500 and hopped a flight into Fairbanks, hoping to buy a small flyable machine. A rude awakening awaited me. In 1980, my savings could only buy a balled up pile of tubing behind a hangar on Phillips Field, a pile which I was not convinced had ever been an airplane.

I headed back to the village frustrated and disappointed. In the next few days, I thought of different options, all based on the fact that since I'd never acquired anything in working order before, why start now. Although rebuilding a plane did seem a little over my head. I constantly reassured myself that even if I owned a functional aircraft, there was always a good chance I'd bend it up and have to start at square one.

I'd heard of several wrecks in the area within a hundred-mile radius of the village, and with the help of several locals, plotted approximate sites on a map.

Then I convinced Claire, who owned an Alaskanized PA-12, to take several reconnaissance/scenic flights. Within a week we had spotted all sites except one, and all were either totally inaccessible without a helicopter, or too far gone to justify a trip across tundra and mountains. Last on the list was a Stinson, crashed in the early '50s, twenty-five to thirty miles down the Yukon.

It was cold and gray the February afternoon we searched the wreck's approximate area, criss-crossing a hundred feet above the trees. I crossed off one mile squares. Low on fuel, with daylight fading, we agreed on flying one more wide circle.

A small patch of dull yellow peeked out from a snow berm, looking like a chunk of sno-go cowling from the air. We decided to have a closer look. Claire shot a compass heading while preparing to land on a small lake.

Landing on skis in a puff of dry snow, we jumped out and untied our snowshoes from the wing struts. Compass in hand, we waddled at a jog into the black spruce.

From the ground, the berm looked like there was a school bus buried underneath. A small metal step ladder pointed skyward from this snow-covered heap. I was convinced it was the classic Stinson. Using the snowshoes as shovels, we stood chest deep and dug hastily, uncovering a large, tattered, inverted fuselage.

Claire called a halt. "It's been here thirty years, it'll be here tomorrow. We still have a runway to stomp out."

The lake was too small. Even with building a small launch ramp and snowshoeing the whole runway, her plane's skis trimmed the trees on take-off. Obviously we couldn't return to that lake.

Back in the village that evening, it was time to organize a strategy without advertising too much. We would need heaters, generators, saws, shovels and come-alongs. Stan, a homesteader forty miles to the north, had arrived for the evening. Caught up in our excitement, he offered to help with his large freight sled and disciplined dog team.

The airplane had lain upside down for thirty years on the tundra, its wing's swallowed by the tussocks and ice. We spent several days heating the metal wing structure with portable heaters run by small generators before the ground would release each wing. They were hardly recognizable.

The last several days we were pressured by an early thaw and overflow from a tributary stream flooding the river ice. The four-mile snow-packed trail from the river through the spruce also began dropping out. The engine and prop, mounted on Stan's sled, flipped many times due to poor trail conditions before we got it to the more solid river trail.

After two weeks and many trips to the crash site by dog sled and snow machine, much of the Stinson was in my yard. The last trip we had all the sleds loaded with wings and fuselage, and pulled straight through town.

There was a big pre-dog-race party, and many folks were out socializing on Main Street, most bleary eyed. They came to attention as this convoy of decrepit airplane parts creaked through town.

With the fuselage mounted on sawhorses behind the house, I liked to sit on an old kitchen chair in place of the pilot's seat, and wonder just what style of Stinson I actually had. It sure wasn't obvious.

As friends arrived, I added chairs and welcomed them on fantasy excursions. That spring, I dug through all aviation books available, anxious to see a picture of what a Gullwing Stinson in flying order looked like. When Claire arrived one evening with a folded-up picture of a V-77 Stinson Reliant Gullwing, I couldn't believe that this pile of pieces could ever had looked like the beautiful plane in her photo.

The parts search was on.

Many phone calls and advertisements later, a contact was made in Minnesota. He had what I didn't, all for sale. He was willing to hold the parts until September, while I tried to come up with more money. I came up with enough for the needed parts by making tents, working part-time as a registered nurse and running a small fish business.

I shipped the plane on a river barge to Nenana, where I loaded her onto a boat trailer towed by an old Chevy panel van. On Thanksgiving, Claire and I headed south. Nine days and forty-five quarts of motor oil later, we hit the Montana border. For three months we lived in a big garage with this hulk and Blue was reshaped, recovered, and hopefully, ready to fly. I wished I was legal.

A retired Alaska Bush pilot, Glen Gregory, hopped in and

gave Claire her first Gullwing flying lesson off a Montana wheat field. Glen's preliminary words of encouragement were, "These Stinsons are built like a bridge - only problem is, they fly like one. Anyway, they always get off before they hit the fence."

We knew he liked flying Old Blue, because he often beat us to the airfield.

Several weeks of practice, and we were ready to head home. Anxious and overloaded, we took off from Bozeman, headed for Alaska. I didn't wonder why the cows were all laying down at the end of the field. The folks who came to see us off congregated at the east end of the runway, all thinking we'd decided to taxi back to Fairbanks. About that time, a small speck appeared on the horizon west of the Bozeman Airport. It was us, never climbing much above the horizon. An hour later we landed in Great Falls, ready to off-load five hundred pounds.

"Now," said Claire, "she's fun to fly."

The shiny classic Stinson gathered a crowd everywhere we landed, often instigating tales from the old-timers who had flown in one of Blue's relatives years back. She was homeward bound, making great time. Dawson Creek, Fort Nelson, Watson Lake, all seemed to go by in a blur, and she never missed a beat. We landed in Fairbanks on Easter Sunday, greeted by a small group of friends who then waved us on to Tanana.

Two long days of flying, and I was in Dawson Creek. The temperature was close to 100 degrees at midday. I would take off at 5 a.m., fly three hours, then put down in the evening. The countryside had leveled out, and I had to be more careful following roads: Suddenly they were everywhere.

I found a small airstrip twenty miles west of Edmonton and spent that evening visiting old friends. Up and off at 5 a.m., I was having a hard time navigating. Forest fire smoke from the Rockies covered the valley. I planned to refuel in

Lethbridge, but the valley was socked in. All I could see was straight down.

Luckily Cardston was up on a plateau, with a small paved strip five miles from town. Blue was hot and dripping oil from every possible fitting. The local preacher also ran the fuel depot. If I learned anything on this trip, it was that you don't call a preacher on Sunday for gas. Fifty gallons of car gas cost me over $150.

Then off we went for Bozeman, Montana, with a bit of a tail wind. Late that afternoon, just as we had climbed high enough to clear Flathead Pass in the Bridger Mountains, with Bozeman runway visible through the saddle, Blue began to surge, the engine racing, then slowing. We were sinking. I put the nose down to gain speed and hopefully cool things, looking for a place to land. I couldn't believe we had made it this far, and now we were going in the bushes.

In clear sight of our destination, I flashed back on old Joe Cook and his many rough landings. Still on the wrongside of the ridge, skimming the hillside at tree-top level, the engine began to smooth out. I started breathing again, pulling back easy on the yoke, hoping for power enough to climb out of Bridger Canyon. Inch by inch, we neared the 8,000-foot pass once again, my pulse racing faster than the engine. Bozeman Airport was in sight. Crossing the pass was like escaping from jail. I put the nose down and glided the fifteen miles to Gallatin Field.

As the prop quit spinning, my wife Claire and two-year-old son Chris ran up. I hugged them both. "How was the trip?" Claire asked.

"For a plane that didn't want to come south, she did a helluva job," I said. "Glen was right, she always clears the fence - though the cow elk have to lie down."

Blue went on to become the centerpiece of a museum in Pennsylvania. I hope, however, that the graceful flying Stinson's flying days are not over. Like Joe Cook, I'd hate to think the tough old bird was finished.

A True Alaskan Experience

On her trip north to Alaska, Maryjane noticed the airplanes she boarded kept getting smaller.

The jet from Albequrque wasn't bad; the six-seater Cherokee from Fairbanks to the village of Tanana was a little shaky; "But now this," Maryjane thought, as she stood back watching suspicously while Rick and Kirk stuffed fishing gear into the small yellow PA-12.

Maryjane knew how excited Rick was to be back home and that he wanted to share a truly Alaskan experience. She wanted to be a good sport, but just couldn't see how all three of them could fit in that tiny airplane. The fact that Rick's older brother Kirk was a commerical pilot and flew daily for the local native corporation was a bit reassuring.

Rick assisted, attempting to direct Maryjanes long legs over the control stick as she clung to the overhead tubing then settled into the rear sling seat. Rick squeezed in, wedging himself next to her.

Kirk walked a last minute check around the plane, when he kicked the tail wheel straight the plane shook, Maryjane grabbed Rick's wrist, her eyes doubled in size.

Into the narrow front seat climbed Kirk. Buckling his fighter jet like shoulder harness. He then pumped the fuel primer and hit the starter button. The small Lycominy engine sputtered and came to life.

Rick smiled, his face only inches away. Kirk moved the control stick. Maryjane could see cables move on the floor-boards and up to the wings. She didn't like the idea of seeing the little cables that her life depended on in flight.

The plane began rolling on its fat, spongy tundra tires as Kirk increased the power. They turned onto the runway. The noise was deafening as the plane seemed to almost leap skyward. Within minutes any evidence of civilization was gone from sight.

Maryjane admired the beauty of the land, the snow-peaked mountains, and moose standing in the small lakes below. Kirk followed the narrow Tozitna River, then flew over a ridge to the Melozitna River Valley.

He yelled, "Highwater." She could only guess. Had he seen an old Indian in the woods named Highwater? At this point, anything was possible.

Then he lowered the left wing and circled a small sandbar on the inside of a curve in narrow river. Maryjane's stomach felt like it had just changed seats. She closed her eyes tight. It only made the swirling sensation worse. Half able to focus, over Kirk's shoulder a narrow patch of sand appeared. He was definitely aiming for it.

"This can't be the runway. No way." She waited, hoping he'd pull the plane up level again.

Then Kirk pulled back on the throttle. All was quiet. Tree tops zinged past at wing tip level, then willows on the river bank appeared to reach for the plane. With a thump, the wheels rolled throwing mud up, plastering the underside of both wings.

Maryjane took a deep breath, relieved. "At least they were on the ground." The plane rolled forward, Kirk stomped hard on the toebrakes. The tail swerved, side to side then suddenly the sandbar disappeared as the big tires splashed water onto the windows. The plane finally stopped.

As the window cleared, it looked to Maryjane that they were sitting in the river. Kirk reached back and twisted the door handle. As he calmly undid his harness, he said, "Time to climb out."

And they did: into four feet of bone-chilling water, making for shore with anything they could grab from the plane, throwing the gear onto the sandbar. Kirk yelled, "Grab the tail!"

He and Ricky hung onto the vertical stabilizer, digging their feet in the river bottom, they tried to stop the plane from going with the current. It was no use, the river was inching her into deeper water.

Kirk disappointingly said, "Forget it," and they swam for shore. The plane nosed over, the wings and engine submerged, the tail stood straight up as the fuselage slowly sank into the clear river.

Maryjane tried to stop shaking, waving her arms as the two men stood speechless, staring at the tail of the PA-12 downriver. She could only think, "So this is a true Alaskan experience."

The sun headed for the horizon late that evening, Kirk hadn't returned, we loaded a Cherokee to go looking. Sandy Hamilton ran the local air taxi and was a veteran bush pilot in the interior. A Cherokee is fast and seats six, good for covering ground and carrying observers.

No one was for sure where Kirk might have gone that morning, but Sandy had a hunch and aimed for the Tozitna. We flew low, scouting every sand bar, then climbed over to the Melozi River. It was narrow but very windy with lots of sand bars. Still there was no sign of Kirk's PA-12.

The midnight sun was just about to set, sending long shadows across the tundra. We were heading downriver for the Yukon.

Then Sandy pulled into a tight turn. Just below our left wingtip was Kirks PA 12 yellow tail sticking up out of the river, the plane plastered against the river bank, still in one piece below the clear water.

Fear was suddenly thick in the Cherokee. Sandy circled, then got low and level. That's when he pointed to the smoke rising up from the sand bar upriver on the curve.

There they were, jumping and waving. We all exhaled in relief together. It was clear where Kirk's wheels had left tracks across the bar and rolled into the river.

We couldn't land, but Sandy planned to return to Tanana and get his Super Cub for the rescue. He flew a wider circle to see what approach he'd use later. That's when I noticed the mama Grizzly and two yearlings digging in the meadow. She looked up and began running as we zoomed overhead. The cubs followed.

It was obvious we were herding the Grizzly into the oxbow of the river and right out to the sandbar our friends were waiting to be rescued from.

I tried not to envision the worst. Here they had survived the plane floating away in the river, now their rescuers herd three Grizzlies in their direction.

Hopefully Maryjane enjoyed her true Alaskan experience!

Let's Change Seats ———

Claire had just greased her Super Cruiser PA-12 float plane onto the Yukon River. She always made it look so easy. For months, I'd been a passenger.

By now I was ready to fly, or so I thought. Tapping on her shoulder, I asked if I could taxi to the dock.

Claire shot me a wary look, cut the power to idle, unsnapped her seatbelt, and squeezed between the seat and window. I sprang over into the pilot's seat and gripped the airplane's controls. With her chin on my right shoulder, Claire begged, "Please don't ram the dock."

I was getting a feel for the stick and rudder pedals as we putted toward the landing.

As the plane rocked and turned from side to side, I could feel Claire breathing faster on my ear.

I turned and said nonchalantly, "How about a flying lesson?"

She gave it some thought as she bit her lower lip. "Okay, but you listen and do everything I say."

"Of course, honey."

I pushed the power level forward. The engine wailed and water sprayed as the high-performance Bush plane lurched ahead with Claire screeching behind me: "Forward, forward, push the stick forward ... no, not that much!"

I was overreacting. Pushing forward, it felt as if we might flip over. Pulling back, the tail kept smacking the water. We were rocking from side to side, one float on the river at a time. Somehow we picked up speed and skimmed along the surface.

As the plane leaped off the river, Claire quit breathing on me. Quit breathing all together, I think.

My knees banged together, palms sweated, mouth dry. While the plane climbed, I slowly turned my head and humbly said, "Claire, let's change seats."

"No way," was her reply. "You got us up here; you are gonna get us down." She waved a small club-like pump handle. "If you take your left hand off the throttle control, I'm going to bruise your shoulder." She looked serious.

Banking the plane away from the river, I checked the fuel gauges, hoping I had lots of time to talk Claire back into the pilot's seat.

"Ah, come on, Claire. I don't want to bend up your airplane. Let's switch."

"No way. Head back now. We're low on fuel," she said. "I'll talk you down."

I mixed all my prayers into a medley, then added a few new ones. I hoped to strike a deal with the Boss upstairs; that's when the boss in the back seat cut in.

"Fly parallel to the river bank, a hundred feet out. This glassy water makes it hard to judge height," she said, clipping out her instructions. "Maintain fifty-five miles an hour, and pick a spot straight ahead. I'll tell you when we're on the water. And just as we touch, ease back on the stick, or we'll flip over."

Well, it sounded easy. I took a deep breath. Thinking I'd surprise her, I planned to just ease the plane on the water, as I'd seen her do so often.

Then Claire shouted: "We're on the water! Pull back!"

I yanked the control stick hard, smacking the river with

the heel of the floats. The plane leaped fifty feet - straight up. A thud on my shoulder told me to push forward on the controls, again too much. The sky disappeared. Nothing but muddy river water in view.

In three such touchdowns, my life flashed by, with Claire in the background screeching and wacking on my shoulder. Finally the plane stopped.

I was afraid to look, but I slowly turned to assess the damage. Both wings were still attached, pontoons afloat, tail section connected.

But Claire. Claire was blanche white and looked as if she was ready to leap from a burning building.

"Let's pull over and talk about it," she whispered.

"Glad to, honey."

Kinda Rough Landing ___

Dave was out practicing. This would be his first landing in his newly rebuilt 140 Cessna. Fact was, it would be his first landing in any plane, ever. He wasn't sweatin' it, because he'd ridden along with buddies in small Cubs, and they'd shown him motions. Besides, he'd had a knack for running machinery since he was a kid in Oklahoma.

Taking off was a bit squirrelly, side to side. He only went off the pavement twice.

For the landing, Dave chose a short grass airstrip ten miles north of Fairbanks. He planned to avoid local air traffic - as well as perfect his landings, then return to town landing like a legal pilot.

Five hundred feet high and lining up with the tree-bordered runway, his only thought was, "Wow, sure looks a lot smaller from up here. Not much bigger than a sandbox."

Kids were playing on the strip. Dave did a low pass to clear the strip. Buzzing along ten feet off the ground, kids and dogs scattered to both sides. He felt pretty slick, banked and did a wide 360-degree, lining up on the same approach.

In the corner of his eye, Dave caught a figure on horseback moseying along the side of the runway."

"Ah, I can avoid them, no problem," he thought.

The plane came in fast. Dave knew that pulling back on the yoke would slow the plane in plenty of time. He cut the power and the wheels hit, bouncing the plane back into the air. Then a side gust hit the tail, changing Dave's view from airstrip to trees. The plane had cocked forty-five degrees.

Pushing the throttle in full, while pulling hard on the yoke, Dave thought, "Oh, this plane can hop those small cottonwood trees. I hope."

And it did. Almost.

The landing gear snagged in the treetops, dogging the plane until it slowly mushed down into the branches. Sitting on the greenery didn't last. The plane nosed over and wedged down between the trunks, it's tail straight up.

Dave was okay. He popped out the door, shimmied down a sizeable trunk, and ran out onto the airfield to see how visible his new parking place was. All the kids were lined up at attention, anxious to meet this new neighborhood stunt pilot. The rider was still moseying.

Dave was staring back into the treetops, hand to his forehead, when the grandma on horseback eased past. With a twinkle in her eye, she winked and said, "Kinda rough landing."

Fresh Melon _____

Dave's first flight hadn't gone so well. He and his newly rebuilt 140 ended up perched in the cottonwoods next to a small airstrip on Goldstream Hill north of Fairbanks.

But now, after several months' instruction, Dave was legal. They were now living in Tanana, a small Indian village 150 miles west of Fairbanks. He had traded his wrecked 140 for a nice 152 Cessna.

Dave and his wife Geraldine added much to the local color. He could fix anything from snowmobiles to washing machines. With his heavy Oklahoma accent and loud "Yuk, yuk" laugh, he was easy to find.

Geraldine, tall and fair with her long brown hair and flowered dresses added refreshing femininity to the village scenery.

Even when Dave promised to circle above the village airport, Geraldine refused to fly with him. She had heard his expanded version of that first crash landing just one too many times.

Dave was persistent. Each evening before he'd head for the village airstrip, he'd try a new approach. "Geraldine, do you remember when you stood at the altar and held up your right hand to Reverend Crumbly at the Broken Bow Baptist Church. You then promised for better or for worse?"

Geraldine perked up. "I sure do, Dave Webb, but I don't

remember promising for better, for worse, and for all this airplane-flying craziness."

Off he went to fly another evening alone.

It was Saturday morning, early July. Dave was sipping a fresh cup of tea as he glanced through the two-day-old Fairbanks paper. An ad caught his eye. It said, "Nice and Sweet Fresh Alabama Watermelon." Dave stopped to organize his thoughts: He knew Geraldine missed the South. She'd been talking a lot about home. Village life was nice, but a lot quieter than she had expected.

On the next page was an ad for a tent revival in Fairbanks Saturday and Sunday. Dave decided to give it his best shot.

"Geraldine, do you remember cracking open the biggest melon in Bobby Jo's patch, sitting in that hot Alabama sun and drinking down the juiciest melon in the world?"

Geraldine looked up from her knitting. The thought made her feel like licking her lips, but she didn't do it. She had a feeling Dave was up to something.

He continued, "Geraldine, ya know what I miss most from home? I miss those outdoor revivals. They would charge me up so I could preach for a week without food. Sometimes I just need that enthusiasm."

Dave paused quite a while. Then with a tone of surprise, "Amazing, but right here in this very paper, there is a big ad for fresh Alabama melon at Safeway in Fairbanks. And on the next page is an announcement of a tent revival with Reverend Percy from Tulsa."

Geraldine put her knitting down, looked up with a smile and lightly licked her lips. Dave knew it had worked. She was finally gonna fly with him.

Off they flew that afternoon, following the Tanana River to Fairbanks. Dave landed smoothly at Metro Airstrip and looked over at Geraldine like, "I told you so." She actually seemed to be enjoying herself.

Off they flew that afternoon, following the Tanana River to Fairbanks. Dave landed smoothly at Metro Airstrip and looked over at Geraldine like, "I told you so." She actually seemed to be enjoying herself.

A late night of Hallelujahs, singing and clapping, then Dave was recharged for preaching in the quiet village.

After church Sunday afternoon, their last stop was Safeway for a load of groceries and the biggest melon they could carry. Friends gathered to see Dave and Geraldine off at the airfield.

Dave stuffed groceries in every corner of the small two-seater. All that was left was two gallons of milk and the melon.

Geraldine climbed in the right seat and strapped her shoulder harness on. Then Dave placed the 40-pound melon on her lap and stuffed the milk under her knees in front of the seat.

Metro is a short, narrow runway. There's a thick powerline crossing low off the west end of the strip, and that Sunday a crane was parked off the east end.

Dave chose a take-off to the west. The powerline appeared lower than the crane. He had never flown the plane loaded before, and wasn't sure how much runway he would need.

They waved to the group of friends. Dave pushed the throttle to full power and the plane rolled for take-off with the engine wailing. Half-way down the runway, the small plane was still solid on the asphalt. Dave's eyes widened, sweat appeared on his brow.

Then he felt the lift as the wheels left the pavement. Dave relaxed, but the plane wouldn't climb. It hung 20 feet off the runway, heading straight for the powerline.

For a second, he thought he might dive the plane under the heavy line. There was too little clearance between the brush and cable.

Dave quickly reached over the melon poking the door latch, he yelled, "Throw the melon, Geraldine, throw the melon!" She clamped down with both arms. Looking at Dave as if he had just ordered her to throw her only child out the door. Dave screamed, the veins in his neck were on the surface now. Realizing the emergency, Geraldine forced the door open with her elbow. She reached under her legs with her right hand as her left stayed glued to the melon.

Two gallons of whole milk splattered on the end of the runway. The 152 cleared the high plane line by inches.

Part III

Living on the
Hudson River
New York

A New Dad

I was excited to have a new Dad. Tom was really my uncle, but he was going to be like a dad. My real father had just left Boston on a big Navy ship to go to the South Pole for six months.

Mom, my two sisters, Mimi, three, Mary, one, and I, age 4-1/2, moved in with our Aunt Anne and Uncle Tom in Trenton, N.J. Tom was a lot quieter than my Dad. I knew with a little time he'd get to like me, and we'd wrestle and play catch.

He sure loved his Siamese cats, George and Martha. Whenever he'd watch TV in the evening or read the paper on the back porch, they'd both curl up on his lap. I tried cutting in several times, only lasting a few minutes before I was replaced by two whining, cross-eyed cats.

A week went by. I hadn't made much progress with my new playmate.

Tom and Anne were at work and Mom was downstairs ironing when I was finally able to coax one of those obnoxious felines into the bathroom. This was the only way I could think of to help make George and Martha disappear. It wasn't easy, but I was quick.

Stuffing Martha in, I sat on the lid and yanked the handle. The toilet made the usual gagging noise, only this time there was an added squeal like a fire siren.

Sure hope Mom doesn't hear. The wailing wouldn't quit. The lid bumped as tiny white claws poked out and gripped porcelain edge. I smacked at Martha's hold and flushed again. No luck. Martha screeched her ear-piercing sound as she tried to bounce me off the lid.

Then there was a hard thumping at the door. I could barely hear it over the squealing cat, but the room shook like there was an earthquake. I wouldn't open up. It was Aunt Anne home from work and threatening me with my life. I flushed again, hoping the wet evidence would disappear.

Splinters of wood flew as the door burst open. My now purple aunt jerked me from my perch and dragged me into the hallway as one bug-eyed, soaked cat shot by and out of the house.

The spanking was a rough one. I ate dinner standing up. Oh, well the cat's out of the toilet now, I thought. Uncle Tom avoided me completely after he heard of my cat washing.

Although he was rarely glad to see me, I was usually up early to join Tom for breakfast. He ritually prepared his two sunny-side-up eggs, with a dab of ketchup, before he rushed off to teach math at Trenton State.

This morning I waited anxiously as Tom palmed the bottom of the ketchup bottle for his daily two shots. The three crayons shot out, torpedoing his mushy egg yolks. Yellow guk sprayed across the table. Tom froze, letting the bottle empty itself onto his plate. His lips quivered as he glared through me. I'd never seen a look like that. Fearing for my safety, I slid under the edge of the table.

The smoking toast saved me. Tom jumped at the toaster, stabbing into it with a fork. Sparks flashed as he twitched, stuck a long while before the carbonized toast and Tom were let free.

Shaking his head and waving both arms, he headed for

the garage yelling words I didn't know yet.

I gave Tom a few days to cool off. Then I crept into his study one evening, hoping we could have a truce. Tom ignored me, but I hung in there, showing how I could be a harmless, quiet kid if I tried.

His aquarium was set up low enough that I could kneel on the floor and still be wet up to my elbows. Catching the bigger of the two fat goldfish wasn't easy. I was real proud and waved my trophy high in Tom's direction, still unable to distract him.

Whatever possessed me to stick its slimy head into my mouth and sidle up to Tom at his desk with the fish tail waving frantically, I'll never know.

Tom turned and grabbed the tail. I was jerked forward as he yanked hard. I only meant to tug back, but misjudged, biting the goldfish in half. Uncle Tom spun in his chair. Palming his mostly balding head with one hand, he held the fishtail high in the air with the other. Waving it fiercely as he charged down the hallway yelling, "Anne, Anne, help!"

In two days, the old Plymouth was packed, and we were moving to Grandma's.

Fourth of July _____

Everything that could be blown up, was.

Fireworks had been going off steady for days. We kids had run out of targets in the neighborhood. Almost out of ammo, too.

Burton, Chapel, Squashy and I decided we needed some spare change to reinvest in summer explosives.

Headed uptown, we tried to look like we belonged - chins up, straight-ahead gazes, as if we had an important appointment.

The subway station was packed with early morning commuters. We sat still until the 8:06 pulled in and left with the crowd, then we headed for the pay toilets. Burton, the oldest at eleven, liked to work alone. He disappeared down the hall.

Chapel and I wedged two M-80s behind the comb and aftershave machine, a good source of commuter change after the rush hour. Squashy flicked his lighter and torched the fuses. We tucked in a stall. "KA-BLAM!!" There were combs everywhere, and the place smelled like an Engish Leather factory.

The goods scooped up, we three piled out the door. Then a sonic-like boom shook the whole station platform and smoke poured from the Ladies Room. Out popped Burton, wide-eyed and long-striding with a big white box under his arm.

Scampering up the stairway into daylight, we knew it was time to vacate. Two of the boys in blue were on our tails.

We fanned out, Squash and I slowed down a bit as decoys. It would be easier for us two white boys to fade into a crowd. Packing our plunder, Burton and Chapel hurtled between car bumpers at the stoplight. Burton could clear a cyclone fence with a TV if need be.

Squash weaved in case the guards got frisky with their pistols. Security finally got winded and gave up the chase.

Huffing, we met at the northside fort under the train trestle. The loot totaled five dollars in quarters and a box built like a safe. Burton explained how he hadn't meant to blow it off the wall, only open it using three M-80s. We could hear coins. We took turns beating on the box with a crowbar. We were about to give up when it sprang.

Two quarters, and what's all this stuff? Burton the genius knew immediately and began his lecture.

"These are little mattress pads. Womens put 'em in their high-heel shoes for sore feet. And some ladies use'em when they cut their legs shaving."

"Yeah, that's it," Squashy jumped in. "My sister always cuts her legs shaving and she has a box of 'em."

Dividing them up, we wrapped them around arms, legs and foreheads. Portraying a beat-up war-torn battalion, we began our mile-and-a-half march along the four-lane for home.

Were we noticed. Cars slowed to have a better view of these four ragged, bandaged boys limping along with walking sticks as crutches, for extra effect.

Korea. World War II. We weren't sure. Singing cadence, we finally hit the sidewalk in front of our apartment row. The whole neighborhood was out on the stoops. Adult faces froze.

Mom leaped from the stoop, turning bright red and jerked my arm almost out of the socket. She dragged me into the hallway.

"Mom, I need some ketchup to make this look real!"

She didn't go for it. Yanking off my combat repairs, she snapped, "These are for women and young girls. You don't wear them around town."

"Be a sport, Mom," I said. "You always let the girls play with my baseball mitt!"

Ace Mechanic _____

Good timing, is the only way to explain how I was able to get that rusty old lawnmower engine up to my bedroom. With all the rules that went with living in the projects, it wasn't always that easy to talk Mom into some of my adventures. Deep down she was a good sport, and I knew if I could get the engine running and attached to a bike frame, she might even take a ride. But for now I didn't want to risk her kabooshing my plan, so I decided to build the motorbike in my bedroom on the sly.

I'd work when the apartment was empty. Lay out newspapers, scrape and probe the heavy cast iron engine. Keeping an ear tuned to the front door, sure if I was caught, I'd have to haul the whole pile back to the county dump where I'd found it.

Progress was going well. The bike was almost ready to mount the engine on. I'd made connections in the 13-year old underground network for wheels, pulleys, and a belt clutch, stashing the works in my closet, with the engine under the bed.

Late summer nights, I'd awake to the hum of several minibikes zipping past the apartment, often a flashing red light not far behind in pursuit, encouraging the riders to head off for the storm drains, a good place to hide on a small two-wheeler.

That Saturday morning, Mom and the girls were visiting the Desmonds in the next apartment row. I rushed, putting the final touches on the heavy five-horsepower sitting in the middle of my room.

Not quite understanding the combustion engine, I decided if the crankshaft turned and I could hear a puff when I spun it by hand, it just might run. I couldn't wait any longer. Wrapping the long pull cord around the shive six times, I held the motor in place with my left foot.

With both hands I yanked hard, then all hell broke loose. My heart jumped for joy.

The engine raced at full throttle, leaping around the room. Glad it would run I tried to shut it off by grabbing the spark plug - the shock made my body twitch and shake faster than the motor. Finally able to get loose, I leaped up onto my bed.

The linoleum floor cracked from the heavy pounding of the engine. The thick blue exhaust smoke, encouraged me to make my escape.

I bounded down the staircase, flung open the door. There was Mom with that look racing up the front stoop. She grabbed my right ear and we both went back up to my room.

The small engine still wailed and beat on the floor. We dodged the beserk chunk of steel and pushed the window open. By now, graham cracker size chunks of linoleum were dancing along behind the centerpiece.

We both stood on the bed afraid to get in its path. I wasn't quite sure how to stop it. But confidently yelled for Mom to grab the spark plug. Deep down I prayed it wouldn't bite her, like it had done me a few minutes earlier. I could swear I'd seen the older guys stop their minis that way.

Mom hunched over and carefully grabbed the white ceramic plug. I was wrong again. She and the engine vibrated across the floor in sync for what seemed minutes. Finally breaking free Mom leaped back on the bed, she smacked me hard on my good ear.

We were both afraid to move from our perch, she tried pushing me toward the maniac motor. The engine began to sputter, cough and finally died.

When the smoke cleared, my room looked like a bomb zone.

Glueing the floor pieces back together took almost as long as finishing the mini bike. Without Mom's help, I never would have made it.

Rude Awakening _____

Rose and Bud always slept in.

Their home was an old blue panel truck at the bottom of our local dump.

Each Saturday, Sunday, and on holidays, us kids' first scheduled event was to line up on the hilltop and heave a variety of things at their truck-home several hundred feet below. Lamps, gallon jugs and television sets were our favorites. Anything that had ever been thrown out, we had thrown off the hill.

Rose and Bud were getting harder to disturb. They must be stuffing cigarette filters in their ears. We agreed we needed bigger items. So we rolled large truck tires over the edge.

All this to get Bud to come out in his trenchcoat and boxer shorts, cursing and waving up a storm.

Then we were satisfied and would be on our way. This Saturday, we launched everything available from the hilltop. Several TVs, a washing machine. At least forty-five minutes of non-stop UFOs.

We could not give up. There was smoke from a small fire in front of their truck's bumper - a good sign that Rose and Bud were still home.

We perservered.

Then Chapel hollered from near the front gate, "Hey fellas,

I got a piano!" He'd been digging around under pieces of broken sheetrock. There it was, an old three-legged flat-style piano. Also known as a Grand.

I bet Rose and Bud were still sound asleep when we finally broke loose the sides and rolled the harp to the launch pad. It was heavy, and it took all four of us to balance it up on edge.

Burton and Chapel strummed a Motown tune, harmonizing. Squash and I got the details worked out for building a ramp out of plywood pieces so this mother hummer would go airborne halfway down the ledge.

"One-Two-Three-Don't Blame it on Me!" we sang. It didn't roll like no tire but stayed on edge long enough to pick up speed while binging and bonging. It sounded like the gates of heaven opening, strings popping.

There was a long silence as the piano went airborne, spinning end over end. Then it landed, crushing the top of Bud's home.

Uh-oh. Had we overdone it? We all froze as the hum faded.

Nope. Bud leaped from the van.

We cheered.

No trench coat this time, just bright white boxer shorts with blue flowers. Bud jumped up and down, doing a war dance around the fire pit. Rose was behind him, wrapped in a ragged quilt, chanting and cursing.

We hollered in unison, "Good morning, neighbors! Rise and shine."

20

Pop the Clutch _____

It beat hauling her to the dump, or so Mike thought.

That was how I inherited the old '52 Plymouth on my fourteenth birthday. Mike knew I liked to take things apart. He reassured Mom that the old bomb hadn't run in months, and probably never would; but it could be good experience and help keep me busy.

That evening, we towed the big prune-colored Plymouth four blocks from Mike's apartment into our driveway. It rolled slow. I rode the brake.

A dream had come true. I now had my own car to work on. Spending that night under the hood, I cleaned spark plugs, filters and other items I recognized from my limited experience.

Home early from school the following afternoon, it was time for a test run, before Mom got off work. To help push, I recruited anyone with two good legs. Three couldn't budge the new monument.

Six made all the difference, including two girls in uniforms from the Catholic school across the street.

We pushed the purple beast several miles. Up and down the alley over and over. She'd get rolling, I'd jump in, try a gear and pop the clutch. A puff of black smoke was the best response we got.

I bribed my help with everything, including driving lessons. I couldn't give up, although it looked hopeless and was getting close to Mom's arrival time.

A loud honk from behind us.

Uh-oh, it was Mike, pulling up in his new Impala. With a scowl on his face, he blew a cloud of cigar smoke. In his thick Galway brogue he growled, "Let's get that back in your yard."

He eased forward, lining up the bumpers. I explained how we almost had her running.

Being a sport, he said, "You get in. Put her in second gear. When we get rolling I'll honk. Just pop the clutch. Either way, it goes back in the yard."

He was doubtful. But I knew in my bones she would run.

"Yes, sir. Thanks, Mike." I hopped in, put her in gear and waved my arm out the window, thumbs up. Off slow, we finally got rolling. I glanced at the speedometer. We were going thirty-five mph. Mike's Impala wailed.

I barely heard the honk.

When I popped the clutch, my chest bounced off the steering wheel. Half-dazed and winded, all I could hear was a piercing screech as the heap leaped and bucked. I was surrounded by a thick blue fog.

I thought, "Wow. So this is jump starting. A little rough on the body and machinery."

I rubbed my sternum and forehead. Then all was quiet and still, except for the clinking sound of glass hitting the pavement.

I jumped out, not knowing whether to head for the hills or face Mike, who was bent over assessing the damage. He was bright red from collar to hairline with cigar smoke pouring from all ports.

Mike looked up from his stooped position and growled,

never moving his lips. "You fool, fool! You had it in reverse."

He was shaking. I kept my distance as he pointed to his shattered headlights and caved-in grill.

I could not believe the mess.

But I could clearly read Mike's mind. He thought, "Why, why not the dump!"

Mr. Gillette _____

The cold New York night packed the pigeons tightly on my bedroom window sill. Tick tick ... tick tick tick.

"Enough of that fellas. You can sit an' mumble, but don't peck the damn glass, or I'll ruin your night with my zip gun," I thought hazily as I tossed and turned, trying to sleep.

"MaaCoon MaaCoon."

I could barely hear it in the distance. "Shit, that ain't the pigeons. It's someone pitching gravel at my window," I thought as I popped up. Looking down into the street, I saw two dudes dressed in suits, leaning against a Cadillac, waving up at me. As I banged the window open, an anxious voice clearly called.

"McCoon, it's Danny and Vito. Get a suit on. We'll fill ya in."

"I hope so," I hollered, lowering the window.

Being called McCoon gave me a clue. I earned the name by growing up in the Black neighborhood. When the uptown fair skins wanted me to do something crude, they'd stretch it out, repeating MaaaCoon MaaaCoon, hoping to jack me up for the occasion.

I dug in the closet for a suit, not my best. Striding for the third-floor staircase, I tucked in my shirt, snugged up a tie and practised a line for Mom, in case she was still awake.

I slid into the kitchen, sneaked up and gave her a hug. Mom was wrapped up in a crossword puzzle. She did a double take and said, "Whoa, what's with the suit? You're a little early for church."

"I must have won something, Ma. Danny and Vito are all excited out front. I'll be back in an hour."

"Don't forget you have a big tournament tomorrow. Your sisters and I aren't going to watch you snoozing on the mat. Be back in an hour or I'll be tracking ya."

"Thanks, Mom, you're the greatest," I said, springing for the front door. As I hit the sidewalk, both clowns gave me a one-armed hug and knuckle shot to the ribs saying, "MaaCoon you've been elected, you're our rep."

"Yeah, I'll be your rep right here. I'm not getting into that Jew Canoe if you don't tell me a true story."

Danny started. "It's a one-on-one over in port. We're trying to keep it clean after that bad scene last week." Shrugging his shoulders, palms up, "You know, keep the doctor bills down."

Singing, "You're tuned, you're our man," he delivered another shot to my chest. "Let's go."

I took a deep breath as I climbed into the white leather rear seat, whispering "Me and who?," not really wanting to know.

Vito spurted, "It's Gallo," as if I would be grateful.

"Oh yeah, that's great. Really keeping it clean. Putting me up against Mr. Gillette himself." I was half pissed.

Vito hung over the seat back, his hands in my face. He explained how things had gone bad at the dress-up.

"Some greaseballs moved in on the ladies, couldn't take no for an answer. So the boys wanted to get to it right on the dance floor. Lucky us politicians got together before it got serious. We agreed on a one-on-one. Best man out front. You were unanimous."

"Hey Vito, I was asleep. Make me feel good. What about

Duke or Ski?"

"Naa, MaaCoon. It's your year. You're breaking county records. Don't play dumb."

"Vito, this is different, and besides, I don't like the sight of blood. Especially my own."

He gave me a disgusted wave as he turned forward, exhaling, "Give me a break."

Chauffered in the Caddy, wearing a suit, I tried feeling like a big cheese. It didn't work. I felt more like a human sacrifice.

My heart sped up. I could feel my neck pulsing against the stiff shirt collar. With a side tug on the tie, I could swallow again.

As if to tie my shoe, I slouched forward and began digging frantically under the driver's seat for insurance. All the while I joked nervously with Danny about ruining the suspension in his nice Caddy, if he didn't quit hauling his big women around.

He was speeding, rocking us side to side on the corners. My left hand found a handle. I eased back, sliding the object up to my lap. The flick of a street light revealed a two-bladed eight-inch paint scraper.

Quickly I slid it into the pocket under my lapel, not wanting to be seen as it was agreed this was gonna be a clean act. I breathed easier as we rounded the last corner of a three-mile ride that felt more like three hundred. The dance hall came into sight. Danny hit the brakes, sliding the Caddy into the curb, almost putting me over into Vito's lap.

Immediately the car was surrounded by our gang cheering."MaaCoon." I stepped out real cool-like, saying, "Hey Pres, this ain't Caesar's Palace." I was sweating as if someone had jammed a lawn sprinkler up under my shirt.

The two gangs stayed at opposite ends of the car lot, chanting "Gallo - MaaCoon." The Aristocrat President Tommy Salerno, their rep Tony Gallo, Delta Pres Danny and I wide-strided it toward the closest alley, two blocks east.

The two Pres's in the center, with me on the inside and Gallo on the curbside, strutting and mouthing about his hands being deadly weapons and how he couldn't be held responsible for the damage they did.

I reached behind the two Pres's and poked Tony, interrupting his monologue.

"So, this is gonna be a clean one, huh, Gallo?"

"Yeah, yeah, you got a problem with tat?" he whined back at me.

"No problem at all. I'll have Danny hold my piece and you can give yours to Salerno." His eyes tripled in size as I slid the scraper out of my lapel. Danny didn't look too impressed as he recognized his own scraper, and reached for it. "Not until Tony hands over his sticker." I made like I was returning it to my pocket.

"Man, I don't need no tool - I got these right here," he extended his arms and flexed his fingers.

"So what's that in your hip pocket, a rabbit's foot?" I said sarcastically.

"Oh, I forgot about that, man. I don't need it for you." He slid out one shiny stiletto and handed it to Tommy.

That was too easy. I knew he had another. As we turned into Duck Alley, I whispered to Danny, "No boots."

Gallo started to dance around, high-kicking as if I would forfeit just from his exhibition. I had seen too much damage done with pointed Puerto Rican fence climbers. Danny stayed in between us with spread arms, saying, "No fight until the boots are off," like it was his idea.

We each took a seat on the curb and with help, removed our high-top shoes. I glanced over and said, "Hey Gallo, you got two ankles on your left foot?" I poked at his sock. "Danny, he's got a straight edge."

Tony leaped up and whipped off his shiny leather coat. "What is this, Customs? I told you I don't need no tools, so lighten up." He ranted.

Salerno stepped forward, hand out. "Gallo, I'll hold it for ya."

"It was a gift from my Uncle Vinny," Gallo whined as he slid a fancy ivory-handled straight edge from his sock.

"Some toenail clipper." Haggerty volunteered.

Standing barefoot on the wet cement, I was numb to the knees. A cool, light fog had blown in, putting haloes around the street lamps. I was hoping for a wrestling tussle. I twisted out of my suit coat and pitched it to Danny.

Before I could turn and ready myself, two solid, stunning shots hit my jaw. The thick taste of blood and tooth chips backed me up. I spit and tried to focus, expecting a flurry of punches that didn't come.

Gallo stood back, contorting his face. He grunted more threats. He should have stayed with it, I thought.

With an adrenaline surge, I started to shuffle and duck to avoid his now-flailing arms. Tony connected several more that I was able to roll with, so they didn't phase me like the first round had.

I hoped for a takedown, then he snapped a kick for my groin. I turned to the side and his foot nailed my hip. "Anything goes," I thought. I was one pissed-off Irishman.

Rallying in close, I faked for his head. When he lifted his arms, I planted a round of solid sternum shots to his chest. A garlic aroma became thick.

I dove for his legs, and drove back until we bounced off a brick wall and onto a rack of clanging garbage cans. Into the gutter we rolled as Gallo hammered on my ears and neck.

Headlights glared as a car accelerated up the alley, then screeched to a sliding stop on the wet pavement three feet away. I saw the number on the door, and thought, "Great, the cops are here. It's over."

The officer shone a flashlight in my face, while we rolled,

grunting and cussing.

"Hey, who's in love tonight?" was his first question.

Haggerty volunteered. "It's McCann and Gallo." The flashlight went out.

"We'll be back in twenty minutes. Let us know how it turns out."

The tires squealed as they sped off. I thought it was a joke. But the police were gone. We continued rolling around for what seemed like an hour - neither was gonna give up.

I could make out a shiny puddle over a clogged drain a few feet away. Hoping a little humilation might help, I dug my toes into the pavement, pushing Tony to the water's edge.

"You're going swimming," I promised.

"My asthma, I can't breath." He was puffing hard now.

"I'm not letting go 'til we have a truce, Gallo." Salerno and Danny hovered overhead. "McCann, don't smother him." Danny was in my ear.

"Truce, truce," Gallo grunted. I jumped up, expecting the worse but Tony slowly stood and put out his hand.

"Good fight, McCann." I expected a punch but he didn't take it. Our backups cleaned us off and helped arrange the clothing.

We walked toward the street. I felt I'd gotten the worst of it - a chipped tooth and salami lip - but could see his pride was drooping. Until we stepped under a street lamp within sight of the gangs in the parking lot.

He came alive, arms flailing again, tongue flapping.

"Now we can take on anyone," he directed. Closer to the crowd, Tony announced, "It was a tie."

Danny elbowed me in the side, "Glad ya didn't hurt him McCoon."

"Danny," I slobbered over my fat lip, "I didn't get off too light myself. Feel like I've been to a drunk dentist. I gotta get home - appreciate the workout."

"No way," Vito said as he headlocked me. "We're buying

you dinner."

"At midnight! Where to?"

"White Castle," Danny said with a smile. "Where else? They have the best nineteen-cent burgers in New York."

"I'll take a rain check, fellas. But how about a ride home?"

Mom was still awake as I slipped into the house.

With a look of concern, she asked sternly, "What did you win, a ride in a cement mixer?"

"I wish. More like a dance with an Italian windmill."

"Did you give him the first shot?" she said, knowing well that I did.

"Oh yeah, Mom. I let him have the first ten! But it was more than worth it. I got a rain check for a dinner at White Castle."

"Nothing like going first-class," she chuckled.

.

The Most Beautiful Girl in New York

Valerie was the most beautiful girl on the island, to me. For eight winters we had skated on Whitney's Pond, never saying a word to each other. If I gave chase after her, playing tag, my knees wobbled, until finally collapsing I would slide past in some embarrassing form.

It's no wonder, that on that June evening when my sister MiMi stuck her head under the old Plymouth and said, "Hey greaseball some poor girl named Valerie is on the phone, she must have dialed the wrong number." I knew she was only teasing and didn't appreciate her warped humor. I was waiting a call from Garcia, I grabbed the receiver and said, "Alright Garc lay it on me."

It wasn't Garcia, but a soft voice - she sounded almost transatlantic. Valerie invited me to her Senior Prom in two weeks. Just checking, I switched the phone from ear to ear. It seemed like hours until my voice returned. I hastily agreed, hoping there was something I could sign to confirm the date. Then I stuttered trying to ask her out next Friday night. Somehow she got the message.

After a long week, I arrived at Valerie's front door. She lived in a quiet Polish neighborhood, the last house on a dead end street. I felt the stares of her neighbors and relatives peering through thin porch curtains.

Last minute doubts rolled through my mind at lightning speed. I tried to look confident strolling up the slate walk. If this was a set up. I had plans. If she looked surprised I'd make a run for it knowing it was the prank I suspected all along.

Could this really be the same Girl that made me a loyal ice skater all those years?

I knocked lightly on the heavy wood door. Then heard footsteps, I was ready to sprint. But Valerie's smile, confirmed I was supposed to be there. She looked tops! In a beige jumpsuit her bronze skin glowed. She stepped aside to introduce me. Her parents stared as if they had recently seen my face on a WANTED poster. I almost caught pneumonia from their handshakes. We assured them that we'd be back by eleven.

I backed off the narrow porch into an ancient rose bush. Val tried not to laugh as she attempted to help release my new shirt from its thorny grip. Free at last, we walked toward Main Street. Val chose Italian dinner, so we headed for Gino's.

In the restaurant's dim flickering candlelight I could barely read the menu. About to complain or find a lightswitch, I looked up.

Valerie's big brown eyes reflected the tiny flecks of candlelight. It was like looking into the Milky Way. That's when I realized the candles weren't put there to save money on electricity. All the candlelight in the room seemed to dance in Valerie's eyes. Her long auburn hair draped both shoulders, then disappeared below the table.

Dinner had never been quite like this!

We ordered Heroes, then talked about Saint Marys and all the nuns we had in common over the years. I ate as slow as possible. Afraid to go to the rest room in case this was all a dream. Then the waitress cleared the table. I wanted to order another dinner so we could stay. But doing quick math, it was clear my five dollars barely covered the tab. This part of the dream was obviously over.

The new movie "Woodstock" was playing at the Corner Theatre. A long line had formed in the spring rain, waiting for the nine o'clock show. By the way Valerie asked if I'd seen it yet, it was obvious that she'd like to go. I dug deep in my pockets, hoping for a cash miracle. No luck. I scanned the line, looking for a quick loan. I couldn't tell her I was broke.

I knew if we didn't get in, the night was over. A walk in the rain can only last so long - especially on the first date.

Casually, I said, "Val I know a short cut."

Valerie hesitantly followed me down the narrow side street. I said a quick prayer to myself, then the right words came straight from Above. I convinced her to stand on my shoulders, and grab the bottom rung of the fire escape ladder. If she could hold tight, I hoped I could pull down enough to raise the counterweight and lower the ladder.

Rizzo was our regular man, it took three to lift him up to the ladder. Then we'd stand back and he and the ladder would come down like a rock.

I pulled hard on Val's ankles, almost lifting myself off the ground. The ladder slowly inched down. I glanced up the alley to see a policeman twirling his night stick one hundred feet away on the corner. He was looking away, but I knew if he turned, my light blue shirt was a give-away in the dark alley.

"Hang on, Val. I'll be right back."

I sprinted to the corner, asked the officer for the time and made doubletalk as I ushered him across the street and out of view of the fire escape. Then it hit me like an antique manhole cover.

I had just left the most beautiful girl in New York dangling from the fire escape.

This was not a bad dream, but a full-blown nightmare.

Val was kicking frantically, trying to get a toe hold in the old brick wall.

I got another grip on her legs and tried to sound reassuring as I began tugging again.

We finally made it through the window bars of the ushers' dressing room and into our balcony seats.

When the movie finished, the lights came up. Valerie gave me a look she had definitely inherited and said with a touch of sarcasm, "Michael, would you mind if we go out the normal way?"

We made it home by eleven.

Horse Corn _____

It was Steve's first legal day on the road. His dad had given him the keys to the old brown convertible, under one condition: He'd stay east of the city line.

"No sweat, Dad, we'll take a ride out to the Island, and I know - be in by midnight."

Finally someone in the gang had wheels. We could hit all the hot spots in one evening instead of hiking, hitching and hopping trains. We went cruising east on Northern Boulevard, Steve and Don up front, Al, me and Billy in the back seat. It was a cool August evening as we rolled along with the top down.

"Corn, let's clip a few ears of fresh corn," I chanted. "Across from C.W. Post College, the field is ripe. I saw them harvesting yesterday. We can get lots for the folks, they'll love it."

We were only two miles away and everybody liked the idea. It was dark when Steve pulled over and dropped us off with a blanket. We ducked through a hedge row and began plucking the biggest ears of corn on this planet. We fumbled armfuls of the nicest-looking corn any of us had ever seen to the roadside, filling the sprawled-out blanket overfull within minutes.

Steve had returned and pulled the car onto the curb. We four grabbed the corners and attempted to lift - no luck. Dragging my corner, I tripped in a hole, releasing my share of the loot. I grabbed frantically to restore my hold. My left foot tingled from small bites.

"Damn it, I'm in an ants' nest," I hollered. "Hurry, the little red bastards are biting the hell out of my leg!"

Billy reached over to assist me, jerking his hand back. "Oh, shit, they got me!" he screeched.

I smacked my left leg as we dragged the loaded blanket to the car, filling the back seat above the window ledge. We piled on: four in front, Al on top of the corn. Steve wasn't expecting this load, and let us know.

"Ah, come on, it's mostly for your folks. They'll love ya."

"Let's go," encouraged Don as we started home on the Boulevard. I was scratching my ankle, claiming that was the meanest bunch of six-legged maggots I'd ever tangled with.

Al started rolling side to side, shouting, "Speed it up, Steve. They're biting the shit out of me!" As we passed under a street light, I looked back to see the corn and Al alive with swarming...

"Yellow jackets! Blow 'em out, Steve!" He accelerated. I stretched my leg over and helped on the gas. We were going eighty, but it didn't help. The hornets were marching up the window ledges and seat backs, onto the dash - a few were now on the steering column. Steve was smacking at the wheel, which wasn't helping the navigation. Al was trying to climb in front. We pushed him back. He was covered with a yellow coat, screaming wildly and swatting himself.

Now going a hundred, it still didn't help. It made no sense. These little terrorists had magnet feet. Steve hit the brakes and swerved into a Burger King parking lot. Al hung over the side, looking like he was on a small branch over Niagara Falls.

We abandoned the car, and corn rolled from the open doors.

We took inventory of damages. Al's backside was doubling in size. My left leg looked like a boiled sausage. Steve's wrists were more like football knees.

"Get out of my parking lot," the manager hollered, waving his arms as he approached.

"Free corn, mister."

"Nice and sweet, ready to eat," I advertised.

His attitude changed. He was interested, tucking a few ears under his arm. He jumped, throwing the ears down.

"You punks. I'm calling the cops." Rubbing his forearm, he ran into the restaurant. We had used our shirts to sweep the buggers off the seats. Grabbing some loose ears off the pavement, we piled in. Each of us perched with the least amount of body contacting the seat, still three miles to home.

Mom looked up as I walked into our apartment. "So you went visiting the old neighborhood again, and they didn't recognize you, or are you now related to Jimmy Durante?"

Steve cut in, "Mrs. McCann, we got you some corn." He piled my share on the table. I had become very disoriented, forgetting my loot.

Mom said, "Mike, go look in the mirror."

My nose had tripled, my ears looked as if they were about to explode, my hands were so swollen they seemed more like webbed duck's feet. Then the lights went out.

Coming to, the scenery had changed. I was strapped down behind a curtain with a needle the size of a flute stuck in my arm. Also I could see around my nose again. Moaning a little brought Mom through the curtain. I half-opened my eyes, figuring I better not recover too quick or she might be pissed.

"Mom, am I gonna make it?" I whispered, injecting as much pain as possible into my voice.

She said, "Twenty more minutes, and you'd have been in the cooler. The doc counted forty stings just on your left leg. He said you couldn't have been stung worse if you'd stepped on a hornets' nest. I said, "I did."

She said, "Whose idea was the corn, Mike?"

I moaned.

"What Rabbit?" _____

Mike, a handsome, graying Italian gent, leaned against his old yellow taxi as the late evening express eased into the station from New York.

When the commuter crowd thinned, he could see Dr. Hill slowly staggering up the wide staircase from the platform. Mike assisted the Doctor into the rear seat of the old low-riding cab, as he'd done each week night for years.

Mike always took the other customers home first. This gave Dr. Hill extra time to sleep it off, before he attempted to walk up the front pathway and meet his wife at the door.

Several minutes before reaching the doctor's house, Mike would lower his window part way, hoping the cool breeze might help sober up his long-time passenger.

Often Mike had to pull down his wool cap and snug up his collar to keep from frosting his left ear. Meanwhile Dr.Hill snored away peacefully, his head flopping side to side as the worn old cab rocked in the curves.

It was more than Mike could understand. As he drove this man home nightly, the same thoughts replayed in Mike's mind... How could such a well-to-do university professor, with a beautiful wife and three healthy kids, get so obliterated each night that he could barely make it home?

Although he couldn't even remember the last coherent conversation he'd had with the doctor, Mike wished he could offer something more than a long ride home and a cold blast of air.

That cold November evening, after dropping off his last sober customer, Mike headed for the wealthy neighborhood of Strathmore Vanderbuilt, where the Hill family lived.

As the cab rolled along the narrow unlit road that wove among the large estates of New York's richest, Mike slowly lowered his window.

A sudden loud thump against his door startled Mike. He slid the cab to a stop in the wet leaves. Shifting into reverse, the back-up lights shone on a skinny dog sniffing over a large furball lying in the gutter.

Mike backed up fast. Honking the horn, he spooked the dog off.

His flashlight showed the largest fluffy Angora rabbit Mike had ever seen. He reached down and grabbed the scruff of its neck, lifted the heavy critter and shook. It was limp as a rag. "Dead without a scratch," he thought.

Mike was sorry he'd hit it, but glad he hadn't flattened the fat rabbit.

Being the thrifty collector he was, Mike immediately envisioned a large pot of rabbit stew. With both hands he cradled the warm body, kneeled on the front seat and lowered it over the seat back to the floor. Dr. Hill was still back there, snoring loudly.

Mike chuckled as he drove on. How would he explain this one to his wife, Leah? Maybe they could roast him next week for Thanksgiving. He slowly shook his head as he remembered that the grandchildren would be over. He knew he didn't want the challenge of convincing the kids they were eating a four-legged turkey.

Then all hell broke lose in the back. Mike's seat bucked

hard, pushing him into the steering wheel. He quickly pulled over and looked in the rear-view mirror. Dr. Hill's arms and legs were flailing wildly. In the dim light, he looked like a flipped-out octopus.

"Dr. Hill must be having DTs," Mike thought. Cautiously, Mike turned to look in the back. The frantic rabbit was more than alive. It was ricocheting from wall to wall, kicking Dr. Hill in the chest with each trip.

The rear door opened and slammed shut, and the rabbit was gone.

Dr. Hill, short of breath and suddenly wide awake, burst out, "WHERE IN THE HELL DID THAT ... DID THAT RABBIT COME FROM?"

Lowering his eyebrows, Mike hung onto a serious look. With a tone of deep concern, he asked, "What rabbit?"

Dr. Hill never mentioned the rabbit again, and was sober for many weeks after that ride.

Mike was glad he could help.

A tribute,

Thanks, Mom _____

Mom made the Dean's List for the second semester in a row. Each weeknight she would head off to Nassau Community College, studying a full credit load in criminal reform. During the day, she cleaned several big homes on Long Island's North Shore

June 2nd, her report card arrived on her 43rd birthday. Good grades encouraged a summer's break after a long school year. We kids - Susan, eleven, Mary, fifteen, Margaret, seventeen, and I, eighteen, were glad to hear a vacation was in the making.

A trip was planned. Susan and Mom packed up the old Ford Fairlane and headed for Montana, where I worked a summer landscaping job. Mimi (Margaret) and Mary covered the cleaning jobs and apartment while working their grocery cashier positions.

This trip was no small move. Mom had never been off the East Coast, and claimed little experience at reading a road map. Seven days after putting the Big Apple in the rear view mirror, she and Susan arrived in Bozeman, Montana, 2,300 miles west.

After a round of long hugs, Susan explained how Mom had wanted to follow rivers and railroad tracks on the map.

"We almost took the Mississippi and then the Yellowstone. But I kept us on I-90," Sue claimed proudly.

"How do you think Lewis and Clark found Montana?" Mom said with her sly smile. "I was gonna take the old route."

"You made great time, and the car held up," I injected "It was afraid to fall apart - way out there - I didn't push it over forty-five. Four farm tractors even passed us," she said.

For two and a half weeks we camped in Montana and Wyoming. We even pitched our Sears tent among fifty tipis at Indian Days, a Blackfoot Indian gathering in downtown Browning, Montana: two days of nonstop traditional dancing in feathered outfits, gambling and all-out hell-raising by the local residents. Mom's early-morning comment was, "This place isn't much different than the old neighborhood. The only thing they're missing is a good deli. I could use an Entemann's Danish."

She was most impressed by several striking-looking Blackfoot Indian women who rode horseback as part of the sheriff's posse. Mom took pictures of them and said many times, "We could use a few of those ladies in New York."

We camped at the base of the Grand Tetons for two nights. Each morning as the sunlight tipped the snowcapped peaks, Mom raised her cup of coffee in a toast.

"I'm not up to climbing that big beauty, but when my day comes, I plan to spend some time on top."

Setting up camp in Yellowstone, Mom and Sue joked about hoping to see Yogi and Boo Boo, the famous bear cartoon characters, until they found several large bear tracks in the sand next to our tent site. "That one ought to be Yogi's granddad," Mom said.

"Na, I think it's a cub." I took advantage of the fact they'd never seen a bear, but was concerned and didn't rest easy myself, even with my hand curled around a large ax handle that night. In the tent, Mom reached over Susan every twenty minutes, poking me lightly.

"Quit it Mom, I can't sleep with you jabbing me," I spoke hazily.

"I'm just checking." She sounded wide awake.

"Checking what?" I was coming to.

"That a bear hadn't run off with you."

"Mom, they don't sneak around like that - they'll just squash the tent if they want something."

"They better not. I have a knife." I wondered what knife she had. As I pointed the flashlight over, Mom held up a regular butter knife.

"They like jelly on bread," I chuckled. My sarcasm wasn't appreciated.

The next morning, we got a close-up of our first bears smudging our windows with their big, wet noses while stopped at a bear jam. They encouraged us to sleep the next three nights cramped in the car.

After two solid weeks, it was tough to say goodbye. When Mom turned the key, a cloud of blue smoke rolled out from under the rear of the old Ford.

"Don't forget to add oil, okay?"

"When the smoke quits I'll add it."

"Right," she winked and off they went, Susan waving until I could barely see the car.

Damn, I was proud of our mother. It wasn't that summer's 5,000-mile trip in the old Ford. That was a scenic cruise compared to the past twelve years.

When I was six, we were packed and ready to move to Alaska. Several months earlier, Dad had been transferred by the Navy to Delta Junction, 100 miles east of Fairbanks. He went ahead to set up a place for us to join him. Meanwhile, Mom and we three children stayed with our grandmother in NewYork, waiting for orders to fly north.

It was Mom's 28th birthday when Grandma handed her the phone, saying with a smile, "It's Jim."

Mom was a foot off the ground when she grabbed the receiver.

Grandma corraled us three little ones in the kitchen to keep the noise down, giving Mom a chance over a poor phone connection.

In the next peek I got through the doorway, her long slim frame was slumped in a chair, hands to her face. Mom's body tremored as she sobbed loudly.

The phone receiver lay on the floor.

For reasons unknown, our Dad had cancelled the previous plans, we were to stay in New York.

With wages as a nurse's aide, the only place available was a small apartment in a low-income housing project. A tightly packed neighborhood of 400 families, mostly poor southern Blacks who had come north to work for New York's wealthy.

Before moving to New York, we had lived in a small New England town. This was to be a switch.

Several of the local women helped coach Mom through the trials of raising kids without a father at home in a rough neighborhood. At first, anytime one of us came home beat up, she would fall apart. Then she'd want to go out and fight our battles for us.

Mom's approach often would change, especially after what she called "stoop sessions," where the mothers would get together evenings on a back stoop. They'd encourage each other to try different ways of dealing with local problem kids.

For weeks I had come running home after school with a whole gang on my tail. They would meet me, the new kid, at the bus stop. The punches would fly, and I would run for home, bloody and crying.

Mom would rush out and chase the gang off our steps, adding to the scene they all enjoyed so much.

Late one evening, after a stoop session, Mom came in and sat on the end of my bed.

"Tomorrow, if you come running home from the bus with a gang on your tail, the door will be locked." She tried sounding stern, but it didn't sound easy for her.

"Geneva and Marie have convinced me that if you don't learn to defend yourself, and I'm not here sometime, those punks will kill you. I can't fight your battles anymore."

"Yeah, Mom. They won't chase me tomorrow," I reassured her.

The next afternoon when I jumped from the bus, the usual gang was waiting. I ducked and wove, but found myself in the center getting punched and kicked. Head down, I barged my way out and beelined for home, my sanctuary. They were all right on my trail.

I leaped the steps, and spun the knob - it didn't turn. The door was locked. I looked up. Mom was half out the second-floor window. I was dragged off the stairs. Tears were streaming down her cheeks.

"Please, Mom," I screamed. "Help!" They were on me, realizing I wasn't gonna get rescued this time.

I don't remember, but was told that I went beserk. The next thing I knew, Mom was pulling me off a kid whose neck I had clamped over a chain fence ten apartments down the row.

The gang didn't meet me at the bus anymore.

Mom called it lesson number one of the ghetto. You have to let them know you're crazier then they are. Then you're considered okay. It held true with some of the adults, and when she had to, she could swing her long-strapped purse like a deadly sling.

The first year was a long one. Finding out who she could trust and count on was difficult. Mom learned to stand her ground, which wasn't too hard when she caught someone stealing her children's clothes off the line.

Anytime she heard or saw an ambulance, she would panic, then run up and down the apartment rows until she located all of us kids. One day, she heard seventeen sirens.

Of the three of us, Mary was the shy and timid one. Mom worried about her, constantly reminding Mimi and I to protect our little sister. Mary was like St. Francis of Assisi. All the animals would go to her - she was always bringing home kittens and pups or squirrels, usually beyond repair. Mom would give them a thimble of scotch to ease their pain. Most rarely made it through the night, one of the side effects of living near a four-lane highway.

Then Tripod showed up.

He appeared on our doorstep early one spring morning. He was a jet black hound, long-bodied and short on limbs - minus a leg, a tail, one eye and half an ear. Mom said, "Wherever Tripod came from, he must have left in a hurry."

Since most of the local punks were afraid of anything with fur and more then two legs, we welcomed Tripod as Mary's friend and bodyguard.

Pets were illegal in the Projects. You could be evicted if caught with one. Mom often let Tripod sleep under the kitchen table, hoping we might not get in as much trouble if caught with only half a pet.

For Mom, the hardest part of living in the Projects was not the squeezing into an apartment with neighbors wall-to-wall, or the crime or violence, but having to deal with the so-called better-off folks outside the Projects.

We attended a Catholic school, where some of the nuns constantly reminded us of where we lived. When we made friends, the first question from their parents was, "Where do you live?" You learn to be very vague. Many times I was offered a ride home and would direct them to a nice neighborhood, where I would point to a house, bail out and run through a stranger's yard, often making my walk home that much farther. Just as long as my new friend's parents didn't know where I lived.

After being honest and letting them drive me home, I'd

wait for the next request, which often was that you not associate with their kids.

When Mom would ask me about a friend I hadn't heard from in a while, I'd say, "Ah, I really didn't like 'em anyway," not letting on that his parents had cut us off. But she knew, and it hurt her to see her kids rejected because of where they lived. She only wanted them to have a fair chance.

Eight years went by. Mom was cooking for the priest at the rectory next to our school when she noticed a vacant, overgrown house across the street. She was able to locate the owner, a rotund Italian chap who agreed we could fix it up and rent it for five years. This would give all of us kids time to finish high school.

Amen. That was our break. We overhauled the place. Fourteen rooms and a yard. Mom had a garden, her own room and walked across the street to work. We had extra space for friends who were crowded out of their own homes. We could be dropped off at our own front door without being ashamed.

The place was always full of kids. Mom didn't mind. Many had come to see her. She often said, "Adults can be so boring, I'd much rather spend time with you delinquents."

Her prayers were answered. Mom always had a distinguished walk, head up, long strides. Now it seemed she held her head even higher and barely touched the ground. We all pitched in and bought a Jeep station wagon. It was always full, heading off to the beach or to visit our extended family from the Projects.

Two great years flew by.

Then one day I ran home from school at noon. Mom was in tears at the kitchen sink. "Oh, no, this has got to be a big one," I thought. Hating to ask, I got out a, "What's up, Mom?"

"The landlord called. He said we have thirty days." Her chin dropped into her chest.

"But why? How could he?"

"He said he has to sell. They're gonna tear the house down for a parking lot." She leaned against the refrigerator. Head down, her black hair stuck to her cheeks.

I hadn't seen her like this since Dad left. I tried to reassure her that we'd find another place, but I knew our chances were slim.

Thirty days flew by.

Apartments were well out of our range, never mind a house. It looked like we would have to go back to the Projects. Mom refused.

As soon as school got out, we held a yard sale and sold everything we could, then gave the rest away except clothes and two beds. We loaded up the Jeep and headed for New England, landing in the town of Keene, N.H..

We rented half of a big old house, then set up camp with an old door as the kitchen table and several electric coffee pots as a temporary stove. Mom's only complaint was early mornings, when she went to pour a cup of coffee and often got a cup of peas or oatmeal from one of the three pots. She called it the Russian Roulette School of Cooking.

During that time, Mom worked as a secretary for an accountant. Evenings, we loaded up the car and explored the countryside. The local pace was a lot slower than New York, and a nice switch for all of us.

I was a senior, getting poor grades, but still hoping to get a shot at college. I received little encouragement from the guidance department. After Christmas, I packed up and hitched to Long Island to finish up the school year, hoping to increase my chances of going on to college.

In New York, I was invited to stay with the Izzo's, a close friends family in Plandome. Mike and Leah Ruggierio made sure I ate on a regular basis between school and work in the evenings.

Dr. Charles Goddard, my new social studies instructor took

a serious interest assisting in my attempt to get into college. Rejections were all I received until late that spring I was accepted by Montana State University and received a full scholarship. It was years before I found out how great a role Dr Goddard played in making sure I got a chance.

Mom drove down for my graduation in June. The trip also confirmed her feelings about moving back. She said, "Keene was a nice break - kinda like being at camp for a year.".

With luck, she found an apartment on Main Street. The girls were happy to be back in New York, regardless of how cramped the quarters were. When the apartment was full, we shimmied up an antenna pole in the air vent and slept on the roof.

Mom cooked part-time at the priest rectory. She kept the curtains closed on the west side of the kitchen to avoid seeing the parking lot of shiny new cars, where our big house stood just a year before.

The girls enrolled back in Catholic school. I went out to Montana State.

Margaret was accepted to St. Joseph's in Vermont the following spring.

That fall, a dream came true. Mom started night school. Each evening Mary and Susan anxiously waited to hear stories about her favorite classes.

It was Thanksgiving, two and a half months after Susan and Mom made the drive cross-country to visit me in Montana when I received a letter. It said she needed "a DNC (women problems)."

"Don't worry, it's a twenty-minute procedure. The doctor at the clinic says he'll get me in soon."

Her letters were always positive and funny. I knew she was worried. This one was different.

When I called home that evening, Mom reassured me, "It's

not a big deal, twenty minutes. Dr. Goldstein said he'd fix me on a Friday, so I don't miss many classes. Please don't worry. Most women in their forties get a tune-up."

She quickly changed the topic to the girls and their latest adventures.

I felt better and told her I had a ride East for Christmas, so she shouldn't worry about me hitching. Then I hit the books for a long two weeks before finals.

My tests were over earlier then planned. I hitched home rather then wait for a ride. Luck was with me. I arrived home in New York two days earlier then expected.

Mom gasped when she got home and saw my old coat hanging in the hall. A nice welcome.

Mary had dinner made. As we sat down to the table, I quickly asked how the hospital procedure had gone. Without looking up, Mom informed me that the doctor had been too busy and unable to see her. She rarely avoided eye contact. I knew she didn't want me to read her eyes. We eased through the meal talking recent trivia.

After the girls went to bed, and the apartment settled down, Mom explained that she had been bleeding extra heavy for six months, that the doctor at the clinic had told her it was very serious, then put her off for over a month.

"I know he's a very busy man," she said, defending his delay. Then she added, "If I could only afford my own physician." She was tired of waiting, all because she didn't have the money.

Her books were stacked against the wall on the kitchen table. Each evening she'd cover its entire surface with notes and graphs. Then we'd stay up late discussing anything from rice to race relations. It was good to be home.

Tuesday night I returned from a friends at 10:30, walked into the kitchen and froze. Mom was sprawled out, face down on the floor. She looked pale and her skin was cold. I felt a pulse, but could not awaken her. I lifted her long, thin frame and sidestepped down the narrow hall to the bedroom and placed her on the bottom bunkbed.

At breakfast she looked fine. I thought maybe the previous night was a bad dream. When I mentioned it, she tried to reassure me that she was just over-tired and must have fallen asleep studying. I went for a long run at the track.

Friday night I came home and couldn't get the bathroom door open. Mom was out cold on the floor. I squeezed through and attempted to wake her, putting a cold cloth to her face.

No response. As I carried her to bed, I ranted about doctors, clinics and waiting.

Susan awakened and leaned over from the top bunk as I tucked Mom under the covers.

"Michael, don't be mad. Mom's afraid."

"Susan I've picked her up off the floor twice. What the hell is going on?"

"She's afraid she's going to die." Those words hit me like a truck. I grabbed hold of the bedpost to steady myself. Finally in a whisper, I said, "She's not dying, Susan."

My first words that morning were "Mom, you've got to see a doctor." It was Christmas Eve, and she said she'd go after Christmas. I was confused. How could she be so with it in the mornings, then unconscious at night?

That afternoon Susan, a friend Valerie, and I went last-minute shopping. On the way, we stopped in the hospital. At the front desk, I asked to talk with Dr.Goldstein. Luckily, a lady named Mrs. Wansa in Medical Records knew Mom and made every effort to help. She put me through to the doctor on the phone.

I introduced myself and said, "Doctor, Mom keeps passing out on the floor. She's never been like this."

Abruptly he cut in. "There's nothing you can do. I told her I'd call her in. Leave it to me."

"But you scared her six weeks ago, then put her off."

Sternly he said, "Monday, two days from now, the day after Christmas, I'll call your mother in."

"Doctor, we are counting on you, thanks."

At dinner I said "Mom, I talked to Dr. Goldstein." She lit up. I tried to control my excitement as I explained how he promised he'd call Monday, the day after Christmas, that he hadn't forgotten her. He'd been busy, and she was next on the list.

It felt good to be able to stick up for her. We had a quiet Christmas. A few friends stopped by. On Monday I went into the city. Mom stayed home, waiting on the doctor's call. When I returned at 7 p.m.. I knew by her look he had't called.

"I am going down there tomorrow," I started.

"He probably had a emergency come up," she said.

"Always covering for the other guy," I thought.

The next morning, I was ready to make a call on Dr. Goldstein when Mom said, "Please, I'm feeling much better. Don't bother the doctor. He'll call."

That whole week, Mom seemed totally recharged. She didn't pass out at all, finished her school papers early and did lots of visiting with old friends. The only noticeable difference was how reminiscent and sentimental she would get late evenings. She talked about the eight years in the Projects and how close you can get to some people during tough times. She talked late about how well all of us had done, how much she enjoyed being with kids and wished she had six more like us.

My report card arrived. I'd earned a 3.2 grade point, my best ever.

The doctor didn't call all week.

On New Year's, Mom, with a carload of my sisters and friends, drove me to Kennedy Airport to catch a flight West. At the ramp gate, after a round of hugs from the gang, Mom stood close and pulled a small piece of paper from her shirt pocket. It was my report card.

"This means a lot. I was always afraid they would convince you." She said in her low-key, very direct way.

"Convince me of what, Mom?" I asked with a grin, knowing well what she meant. She choked up. "That you couldn't do it, and I knew you could." I gave her a bear hug and turned to enter the ramp to the plane.

I awoke at 6:45 the next morning in my cabin, ready to go register for classes. While fixing breakfast, I felt gravity had tripled its grip. It was an awful feeling, dark and heavy. I staggered, then laid down.

Two hours later, a knock awoke me. It was a good friend, Carl. He didn't talk, but tried to put his arm around me. I knew for sure.

"Don't say a word, Carl. Don't. She was all we had. ALL WE EVER HAD."

I went raving mad, smashing anything I could get my hands on, as the past eighteen years flashed by. Carl waited until he could get close, and hugged me.

I had lots of time to think before getting off the jet in New York. My feelings tumbled over and over.

Mom had run a marathon all her life. I was relieved that she could rest now. But she had made it to the the finishline, only to be tripped. She had beaten the rap, still young and full of life. How could she be gone forever. And what about us kids? Susan was only eleven.

Uncle Tony met my flight. I raged how Dr. Golddigger scared Mom and then let her bleed to death because she couldn't contribute to his Cadillac fund. I was livid.

The first stop was to pick out a casket. I also requested several rooms for the service. Mr. Fliedner, the funeral director, said the place was ours.

Each evening hundreds of teenagers and youngsters arrived

to say good-bye. There were many adults too, but what stood
out were how many young people came to share our pain. The
many bouquets of flowers that lined the walls had cards that
read, "From the Gang in Keene, St. Joseph's and St. Mary's."
It was obvious where so much of her energy and love had
been shared. She had been a Mom and a friend to many more
than her own children.

As one close friend said when I helped him to the door,
"You guys were sure lucky. You may not have had her for
long, but you sure had the best."

That's how we feel, and for this we are grateful.

Since our mother, Kathleen Rudden, passed on, I have flown
my small airplane high up next to the peak of the Grand Teton
several times. I like to remember her during her trip West when
she was sitting next to the morning campfire. She toasted the
mountain with her coffee cup and said, "I'm not up to climbing
that big beauty. But when my time comes, I plan to spend
some time on top."

On one flight, I took her first grandchild, Christopher, along.
We circled several times, waved our wing tips, then flew home
under a rainbow.